Making Phaser 3 Collapsing Blocks Browser Games

Stephen Gose

Making Phaser 3 Collapsing Blocks Browser Games

Creating "Same Game" Mechanics for Phaser.js Gaming Frameworks v3.16+

Stephen Gose

This book is for sale at http://leanpub.com/mbg-collapse

This version was published on 2020-10-16

Leanpub

* * * * *

This is a Leanpub book. Leanpub empowers authors and publishers with the Lean Publishing process. Lean Publishing is the act of publishing an in-progress ebook using lightweight tools and many iterations to get reader feedback, pivot until you have the right book, and build traction once you do.

* * * * *

ISBN for EPUB version:

ISBN for MOBI version:

For my students

@ Culpeper Public Schools, Culpeper, VA;

@ ITT Technical Institute, Tempe, AZ;

@ Early Career Academy, Tempe, AZ; and

@ University of Advancing Technology (UAT), Tempe, AZ

Table of Contents

Supporting website

https://makingbrowsergames.com/p3gskc/

Disclosures

- ***Stephen Gose LLC reserves the right, at any time and without notice, to change modify or correct the information contained in this publication.***

- I refer to "Phaser v3.16+" under a ***moniker of "Phaser III"*** to distinguish it as a clear demarcation from previous versions.

In this book, I am not paid to recommend any of the tools or services presented but I do use affiliate links. Here's how it works. When I find a tool, service, author's content, idea, or product I admire, I investigate if they have an affiliate program. If it exists, I get a special link and when you click it or confirm a purchase I receive a small percentage from that activity. In short, it's the same methods everyone finds on any typical website; only now, those reference links are available inside ebooks and is a ***substitute for "crowd-funding" websites.***

I think everyone, with *any business savvy,* should do this too; especially when you recommend books, services, and tools to your own products. Amazon and other publishers offer affiliate links. Whenever you recommend anything **(hopefully this book? hint, hint!), use your affiliate link.**

By law, I must disclose that I am are using affiliate links. Amazon, in particular, requires the following.

> *"We are a participant in the Amazon Services LLC Associates Program, an affiliate advertising program designed to provide a means for us to earn fees by linking to Amazon.com and affiliated sites."*

Thank you for your patronage! I truly appreciate it.

Disclaimer

- All the information, contained within, is for the convenience of its readers. It is accurate, as can be reasonably verified, at the time of original publication. However, this content may not reflect migrating industry recommendations *after the original publication date* for *ECMA-262* (also known as *(aka)* "JavaScript", ES5, ES6, ES7, ES8, ES9 or ES10) or for any versions of the *Phaser.JS Gaming Framework.*

- All websites listed herein **are accurate at the time of publication but may change in the future or cease to exist.** It is best to research these "dead websites" links in *"The WayBack Machine".* The listing of website references and resources does not imply publisher endorsement of a site's entire contents.

- There are no guarantees nor warranties stated nor implied by the distribution of this educational information. Using this information is at the reader's own risk, and no liability shall carry to the author. Any damage or loss is the sole responsibility of the reader.

Warning: The Phaser newsletter dated 21 September 2018 includes projected development on Phaser v3. In August 2017, many features before v3.16.x was removed. There were many business decisions on why they were removed based on financial support and sponsorship deadlines imposed. Phaser v3.14.0 (released OCT 2018) **saw the return of these deleted features.** In other words, Phaser v3.14.0 returns to the original vision of January 2017 after several rewrites. Phaser v3.15+ was the next massive re-write (released OCT 2018); followed by **v3.16.0 DEC 2018.**

My best guess is that *all books, tutorials, and "how-to" articles — written before Phaser v3.16.0 (NOV 2018) — are not fully functional with "Phaser III" (as v3.16+) and should be re-written to meet the Phaser v3.16.0 minimum standard baseline. Hence the reason this book is dedicated and updated to the official Phaser III (release v3.16+) and has removed any references to previously released versions before v3.16+ (See newsletter #139 dated 20190211) for specific "Breaking Changes"*

About this Workbook

This latest edition offers more development tools and production methods which I call the *Game Design System™* in which we'll create *Game Recipes™*. We'll create game prototypes in this specific game genre. Expert game developers understand the "Don't Repeat Yourself" (D.R.Y.) concept, yet few have taken a step back to the "10,000-foot view" on their game production pipelines. We'll do that aerial view in this book as we follow this game's development process and then **"nose dive head-first"** directly into Phaser Gaming Framework v2.x.x **and** v3.16+. I believe you will be surprised how quickly and easily we can build games using this *Game Design System™* with its *Game Recipes™ tools.* This workbook is intended to be a hands-on guide for HTML5 game development with an emphasis on the *Phaser JavaScript Gaming Framework — either v2.x.x or v3.16+.* Yet, our game product and project management could apply *to any game development framework! It's not exclusive to the Phaser JS Gaming Framework.*

Links and References

The Internet is a living, dynamic information resource *that doubles every 35 days! There are several reasons this book points to external content because —*

1. it provides you the "research path" I took to present and develop my ideas. It takes all the guess-work out of it and conserves your research efforts. This saves you 100s of hours of your personal free-time searching for supporting facts and opinions.

2. it avoids copyright infringements and **provides the required acknowledgments** to "Open-source authors" for their contributions and use of their resources under these various licenses **and EULA.**

3. it provides external authors the opportunity **to recant (or update) their published content.** Technology is a fast-moving target, and what was once "cutting edge" becomes obsolete. For example, the use of **"window.onload"** was recanted by its originator back in 2014 as an unsafe method for launching browser applications.

4. it **reduces your initial purchase price** from the reams of "padded source code content" **— don't make me embarrass those authors —** while keeping your investment in this book's information **"fresh".** This book would be double the size and twice the price if I had embedded all of this tutorial's source code as others do.

You'll find your **Bonus content, source code, and references** in —

- the footnotes links,
- external reference links, and in **the various linked files** which are available directly from my supporting website **(without registration nor logon thus keeping your personal information safe!)**
- or from the latest edition updates found in your **LeanPub.com personal library (assuming you are a LeanPub patron).**

All the source code is written in **"pure"** JavaScript (JS) and the **Phaser.js Gaming Framework for both v2.x.x, and III (v3.16+);** it doesn't use any additional "abstraction layers" such as "TypeScript", "CoffeeScript", or "JQuery" for obvious reasons.

I've *"gone to great lengths"* to make this book "skim-friendly" — **even for my International customers** by emphasizing important concepts in bold font type. I have provided links to *"English (American) Jargon phrases"* that will help translate this content directly into your native language. This entirely new edition has more screenshots, step-by-step worksheets, thoroughly annotated source code listings, and diagrams. I use "Notes", "Tips", "Warning" and "Best Practices" icons to encapsulate those ancillary topics for your further education from **other experts** in the gaming industry.

I assume that many readers will want to use this book to quickly build their *bespoke* game developments. So, I've included references to other similar game examples, gaming engines, frameworks, *GUI game kits*, indie developers, authors, their "open-source" contributions, articles, books, *artwork*, application tools, and their wisdom.

Workbook Content

This book will **not** teach you *HTML5*, *CSS* nor *JavaScript programming fundamentals*, game design *allegedly "best practices"*, nor software encoding syntax. **I assume you (the reader) already knows these technologies.**

This workbook does provide simple-to-follow worksheets, step-by-step instructions, and a straightforward-approach to building games **from component prototypes** using the ***Game Design System™*** methods discussed in the *Headless HTML5 Game Design™*, *Phaser Game Design*, and *Phaser Game Prototyping Workbooks*. (No, these books are ***NOT*** a prerequisite; I'll cover the minimums for you.)

All these tutorials are written in a fun, friendly conversational-style with one or more example projects and numerous open-ended exercises that encourage you to include your bespoke game assets and features. You also have access to bonus content, downloads, supporting tools, and source code snippets from this book's website — *https://makingbrowsergames.com/p3gskc/*.

Consider this book as a joint effort in game creation; I take the role of your game programmer while you fulfill the roles of game designer, artist, and marketeer.

How to Read & Use this workbook:

The *"Making Browser Games"* is a series of "single-chapter tutorials" for creating specific game genres using **either** the Phaser 2.6.2, CE, and/or III (v3.16+). Each chapter is part of a larger volume — *the "Phaser Game Starter Kit collection"* — of 16+ popular game mechanics and 19 sub-genres (35+ total!) with development techniques.

Start by reading — or skimming through — the *Introduction Section* so that together we are speaking the same "game references" and terminologies. Then, select the Phaser version — either v2.x.x or III (v3.16+) — that interests you and begin your bespoke game project development.

Here are the topics in this edition:

- Game creation in this genre using both Phaser 2.x.x **and** v3.16+ new features.
- How to integrate specifically focused game mechanics with other game genres — for example, RPGs or Combat Systems!
- Deploy games as either a "Content Management System" (CMS), a "Progressive Web Application" (PWA), or a "Single Web-Page Application" (SWPA) for any device.
- Analyze current market demand for this specific game's genre, where, and how to deploy it.
- Automatically generate various game board environments.
- Instructor Guides and teaching resources available for workshops in the Teacher's edition with online course content.
- Access to *several Free online courses* included with this purchase.

- **Coding Style Appendix:** sections dedicated to interested Senior Programming Engineers and the *rationale on why and how* migration away from classical OOP to OLOO compositions is important.
- **"The Deeper Dive"** sections for interested Software Engineers concerning Phaser Gaming Framework.
- The *"Headless" Game Design System™* development method for Game Software Project Management.
- Each *Construction Section* contains several Parts. It starts with an "Introduction Overview" into the goals, game ludology, workstation set-up, and generation tools. In a matter of hours, you will have a working game prototype for this game genre's mechanics. All that remains to do is to add your own artwork and additional game features; after a few days, you'll have a completed game ready to deploy to any "apps" store.
- You'll find detailed working examples, with dozens of illustrations and many concepts you can freely apply to your own gaming project developments.
- All the source code is annotated with enhanced explanations.

Viewing this eBook:

This book includes programming code which is optimally viewed *in single-column, landscape mode,* and adjust the font size to a comfortable setting.

Who should use this workbook?

This workbook targets both the *learning novices* — those who enjoy "learning by doing" using *"deliberate practice"* — and *experienced expert programmers* in web-application development; and, of course, anyone who wants a finished game from their own designs and efforts. If you are interested in making browser games, *especially for the mobile market,* then this book is a perfect choice along with its companion volumes: the *Headless HTML5 Game Design™, Phaser Game Starter Kit Collection,*

Phaser Game Design Workbook, and *Phaser Game Prototyping*. With this in mind, you will do a lot of writing, thinking, and coding in both HTML5 and JavaScript throughout this workbook. You may prefer using either physical- or soft-paper to organize your development ideas and processes.

This **workbook is a tutorial guide** into the ***Game Design System™*** methods using "full-stack" technologies with **an emphasis on the Phaser JavaScript Gaming Framework — but could be applied to any "Front-end" Gaming Framework.** I know that many *senior software developers* may already have these "full-stack" technologies (i.e., server-side "Back-end", and "Front-end" *HTML5*, *CSS*, or *JavaScript fundamentals*) in their arsenal; but, I have received dozen of *email "back-wash"* (aka "complaints"?) about this book's former editions as being **"… too difficult for those just starting their own game studios." Therefore,** if learning any of these mentioned technologies is what you are initially seeking, then I recommend a visit to either **W3Schools** or *Free Code Camp* as your **first FREE starting point.** By following their instructions, you will learn a complete foundation in HTML, CSS, and JavaScript **in a matter of hours! (just as I did in 1997 from W3Schools!) … then,** return to this workbook and learn how to combine those technologies into your bespoke creations.

In summary, if you are a ***hobbyist, independent game developer, student, teacher, or start-up game studio*** you will find a wealth of information on project management, game design, Game Mechanisms Framework Components (GMFC), Game Mechanics (GM), and "insider's tips" about the ***Phaser JavaScript Gaming Framework.***

Your newly obtained skills...

By the end of this workbook, you'll have integrated into your own *bespoke* game design:

- ***Step-by-step methods converting older Phaser v2.x.x into v3.16+.***
- ***Built "future-proof" and flexible game architecture.***
- Discover the new trends in *"Headless Game Design"*.
- Used the **Game Design System™** which creates *Game Recipes™* from automated tools.
- Adopted processes for software project management using "agile development".
- Organized a standardized file structure for general game developments;
- Used a blank game template to scaffold further game projects;
- ***Converted and adopted new upcoming changes in Phaser III API.***
- ***Managed groups and layers of game objects with Phaser III;***
- Imported resources and game assets;
- Displayed, animated, and moved game avatars on various screen renderings;
- Incorporated sound effects (sfx) and theme music across various game scenes;
- Deployed heads-up display (HUD) on game scenes both inside and outside the canvas;
- Used customized web fonts;
- Incorporated multiple user interfaces (touch, multi-touch, accelerometer, mouse, and keyboard);
- Rendered several physics systems;
- Created and managed various game phase deployments for CMS, SPWA, & PWA;

- Managed permanent game assets across game phases and scenes;
- Optimized your games for various user *IoT gaming devices*;
- Integrated several 3rd-party scripts and services.

Game Design System™

"Game Recipe™" Courses (purchased separately on specific gaming mechanics) using the ***Game Design System™ management method and concepts.*** These courses enhance your skills and are available from my educational websites (*hosted by LeanPub.com*) or *Training By Blackboard, Books, and Browsers*.

You can earn your ***Game Development Certifications*** from *my online courses*, from *Udemy (102-pages of online courses!)* *or Zenva (my personal favorite!)*; to enhance your resume.

Game Studio - Book Series

Learn to build a Gaming Studio for passive (or secondary) income!

- *Game Studio Starter Kit Bundle* — ***Start your own Game Studio for passive or secondary income!*** This bundle shows you how to develop product and project management in the gaming industry from my 23 years of experience. You'll learn how to quickly build game prototypes in any genre, launch, and then distribute your games. You'll also have 16+ popular game genres to choose from for your product line with 19 subgenres to expand upon. Learn how to capture various game industry market shares.
- *Headless HTML5 Game Design (Vol. I)* — Creating Cloud-based **"Content-as-a-Service" (CaaS)** games *for Any Gaming Device.*

- *Making Massive Multi-Player Online games (Vol. II)* — Creating Multi-Player Online games **using the Full-stack, White-labeled, and "Content-as-a-Service" (CaaS) Architectures.**
- *Making Multi-Player Online games* — A Game Development Workbook **for any** Phaser JavaScript Gaming Framework. This book is a thorough review of MMoG mechanics for both client- and server-side APIs using Block-chain, WebRTC, RPC, MoM, SSE, Cloud Services, and Web Sockets (Berkeley). **I do not recommend for entry-level developers;** mastery of several *IT technologies* is required.
- *Phaser JS Game Design Workbook* — 6th Edition for v2.x.x **and** v3.16+ — guidance on project and product management in the gaming industry.
- *Phaser Game Prototyping* — 6th Edition for v2.x.x **and** v3.16+
- *Phaser Game Starter Kit Collection* — 6th Edition for v2.x.x only.
- *Phaser III Game Prototyping* — 6th Edition for v3.16+ only.
- *Phaser III Game Starter Kit Collection* — 6th Edition for v3.16+ only.

Game Studio - Online Courses

- *Phaser Game Design Workshop Course* — guidance on programming your first game in v2.x.x.
- *Phaser Starter Kit Game Collection* for either Phaser v2.x.x **or** Phaser III.
- *Phaser III Game Design Workshop Course* — guidance on programming your first game in v3.16+.
- *Game Studio Starter Kit Collection (basic)* — 3 courses are included in this Business starter kit for Game Studios ... "Making Dating & Quiz Browser games", "Making Online Dress-UP Fashion games", and "Making Puzzle Browser games" with Phaser v2.x.x.

- *Ultimate Game Studio Starter Kit Collection* — 6 course-set are included in this Business starter kit for Game Studios. Build your own Game Studio business for as little as $17.99.

"Making Browser Games" - Books Series

Individual Chapters — **sold separately from the** *"Phaser Starter Kit Game Collections books"* — contain **both** the Phaser v2.x.x **and** Phaser "III" (3.16+) examples, source code, and game license. Find and select your favorite game genre.

Chapter 1 — *Action & Arcade*
Chapter 2 — *Adventure Mazes & Story Plots*
Chapter 3 — *Collapsing Blocks*
Chapter 4 — *Connect 4 & Go*
Chapter 5 — *Dating Simulations & Quizzes*
Chapter 6 — *Defensive Towers* — the typical tower-defense constructions **with two innovative variations.**
Chapter 7 — *Dress-Up & Fashion*
Chapter 8 — *Hidden Objects*
Chapter 9 — *"Jump to Capture"*
Chapter 10 — **MahJong — available only** in the *"Phaser Starter Kit Game Collections"* volumes or the "Memory Match" **mega-chapter.**
Chapter 11 — *Match-3 & Trace 3+*
Chapter 12 — *Memory Match* for Pairs (either "Open" or "Hidden") & Sequence matching — a **"mega-chapter" with 5 games and licenses.**
Chapter 13 — *Music & Rhythm*
Chapter 14 — *Puzzle (both Jigsaw & Sliders)*
Chapter 15 — **Role-Playing Character Development — available only** in the *"Phaser Starter Kit Game Collection"* volumes. *Role-Playing Content-as-a-Service (CaaS)* — a **"mega-chapter"** developing content for B2B, Affiliate Syndicates, and clients is **NOT available** in the *"Phaser Starter Kit Game Collections"* volumes.
Chapter 16 — **Simulations — available only** in the *"Phaser*

Starter Kit Game Collections" volumes.

Chapter 17 — *Strategy & Tactics*

"Making Browser Games" Series - online Courses

- *Making Browser games — Tower Defense* with Phaser v2x.x and v3.16+.
- *Making Dating & Quiz Browser games* with Phaser v2x.x.
- *Making Online Dress-UP Fashion games* with Phaser v2x.x.
- *Making Peg Solitaire Browser games* with Phaser v2x.x.
- *Making Phaser III Peg Solitaire Browser games* with Phaser v3.16+.
- *Making Puzzle Browser games* with Phaser v2x.x.
- *Making RPG Browser games* with Phaser v2x.x.

Programming Courses

See the growing catalog of courses for **college credit, homeschooling, or personal skills development** at *Training By Blackboard, Books & Browsers*

- *Using JavaScript OLOO in game development* (learn JavaScript development)

"Walk-Thru Tutorial" Series - Online Courses

These courses are "step-by-step" guides to create specifically designed games with some explanation as to why we do this (which is typically found in most online tutorials).

- *"Walk-Thru Tutorial Series" - Blood Pit™ (IGM)*
- *"Walk-Thru Tutorial Series" - Blood Pit II™*
- *"Walk-Thru Tutorial Series" - Mozart's Music Match™*
- *"Walk-Thru Tutorial Series" - Rogue Prince Quests™ (IGM)*

Making HTML5 Games

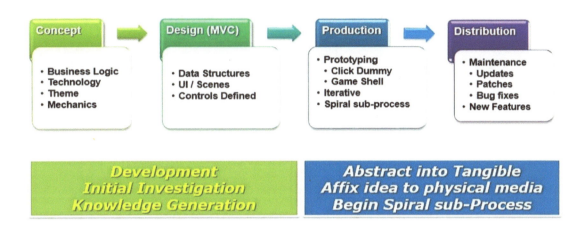

Software Project Management for Games

Affixing your idea to "physical media" secures your Copyrights © as an expression of your idea. Never go public during the "Concept" and "Design" phases. You can publish "multiple expressions" from the same idea.

1 Introduction to Game Design

Approaching Game Development

An Except from "Macromedia Director Game Development" available from *Amazon.com*

Whether you are an experienced game developer, a master of video games, or even new to computers, a great computer game will offer you entertainment and often some type of competition. Over the years, basic games have evolved to encompass numerous genres such as role-playing, first-person shooter, side-scrolling, strategy, educations, and simulations. Role-play games involve a main character or characters thrust into a heroic plot. A first-person shooter, however, involves adrenaline-fed killing and destruction. Although simulations are generally designed to be as realistic as possible, most side-scrolling, strategy and educational games tend to be a bit more simplistic. With the wide variety of games available today, the average person will have no trouble finding a game that suits their desires. As you develop your game design skills, ***avoid simply mimicking existing games.*** In most cases, however, any game you develop will fit clearly ***into a specific genre.***

Focusing Your Game

When you begin the process of designing a game, you must first decide how to approach the task. Determining the focus of your game is the best way to begin. You should decide on a ***topic, purpose, and theme*** for your game. Listing objectives that you want to accomplish through your game is often a smart way to begin. You might have objectives that direct the activities you will build into the game and a different set of objectives for the person who plays the game to accomplish. Through your thinking process, you will determine exactly what your game is about and how you should go about creating it. How you focus your game development **will affect all the decisions you make later in the design process.**

1.1 Game Genre Defined

Game genres can be confusing. The inconsistency comes from trying to describe a game's mechanics, a game's delivery with details associated with the game's theme.

GG Interactive — *Game Design Course*

Genres don't help market a game — instead, the selection of a genre affects what (the size of) audience is likely to be interested and willing to purchase a game. Genres do help an audience understand the basics of a game by promising them a certain amount of familiar elements they desire (or demand) in a particular genre. For example, fans of medieval fantasy will expect some common themes in a ***Fantasy Real-Time Strategy*** (FRTS) game: knights, castles, troop combat, and magic, to name a few. As a game designer, it is important to understand what kind of audience expectations exist across different genres. Stray too far from these expectations without designing a brilliant alternative and the game will lose its audience. Stick too close to what has come before and the game will be overlooked as offering nothing new. Even the bold designer that intends on rewriting all that we know about how a genre game is played, needs to understand what, to this point, has made the genre popular before deconstructing it and making it better.

Exercise: Launch your personal *FREE Game Design course*.

Download Free Bonus Content: "Game Category Classifications Compared"

"Genres are not usually defined by the actual content of the game or its medium of play but by its common challenge." quoted from *(Fundamentals of Game Design)*. The usual challenges are the rules which govern gameplay. Game genres are separate from their interfaces, management operating system platforms. If we turn to ludology (aka **gaming theory**), it classifies games according to several criteria —

- whether a game is **symmetric** or asymmetric,
- what a game's "sum" is (**zero-sum**, constant sum, and so forth),
- whether a game is a **sequential game** or **a simultaneous one**,
- whether a game includes **perfect information** or **imperfect information**, and
- whether a game is **determinate**.

1.2 Game Tools & Generators

You will discover many supporting tools from "MakingBrowserGames" GitHub and in the Appendix of this book. Here are some tools that will help in generating gaming ideas, game design documents, and dynamically generated project source code.

- *Random Game Mechanics Generator* — This idea generation machine randomly selects 3 — by default — common game theory mechanics. The game mechanics and descriptions should help your imagination blend and produce the next blockbuster game.

- *Game Mechanisms (FREE Limited Access)* — This library of game controls and mechanisms spans several JavaScript gaming frameworks. (more are on the way!) This tool helps you choose the game controls then opens the generic code snapshots (aka "snippets"). Spend a minute to re-factor those snapshots to your design and you'll have a functional game prototype within minutes.

- *GIT* — Git is a free and open-source distributed version control system designed to handle everything from small to very large projects with speed and efficiency. Git allows and encourages you to have multiple local branches that can be entirely independent of each other. The creation, merging, and deletion of those lines of development takes seconds.

"Challenge yourself to create a code-base that compiles and runs in the first few hours. **Make it so that you can accept inputs, move around, animate something, and trigger some sounds. This prototype, as lousy a game as it may be, is going to be your best friend. The sooner you can have a working early playable prototype, the more likely you are to succeed.**

No-art prototypes also have one other major advantage: in previous games, I would make beautiful mock-ups in PhotoShop and gather hundreds of lovely looking sprites in preparation for the game. **After development was complete, the vast majority of the art had to be replaced, re-sized, or thrown out. I've wasted thousands of hours making game-ready artwork before coding;** these days I know that the tech specs and evolving game-play mechanics will mean that much of what you make at the start won't make it into the finished game." by Christer Kaitila: *The Chunky-*

pants Method #1GAM: How to Succeed at Making One Game a Month.

1.3 References From

This tutorial is a single chapter from a larger collection of 16+ game mechanics and 19 sub-genres found on http://leanpub.com/pgskc/

- ***Phaser Game Design Workbook***[1] in the newly revised and ***expanded 6th Edition*** in paperback or Kindle from ***Amazon.com*** or ***LeanPub.com***
- ***Phaser Game Prototyping Workbook (6th Edition)***[2]
- ***Phaser Making Massive Multi-player Online Games (5th Edition)***[3]

This tutorial is a single chapter excerpt from the ***"Phaser Game Starter Kit Collection"*** — a compendium of 16+ game mechanics and 19 gaming sub-genres. Bonus Content is available from the supporting websites.

- *https://makingbrowsergames.com/starterkits/*
- *https://makingbrowsergames.com/starterkits/collapsingblocks/*
- *https://makingbrowsergames.com/p3gskc/*
- *https://makingbrowsergames.com/p3design/*
- *https://makingbrowsergames.com/p3gp-book/*

2 Standard Project Setup

Enough "chit-chat", let's create some `file structures` and set-up our development workstation. You could create this project's file structure by creating each directory manually; **OR,** you could use *Yeoman (for Phaser v2.x.x)* or *Yeoman (for Phaser v3.16+)* and generate your Phaser project automatically. If that seems too intimidating, then your best alternative is to download our *FREE*

Phaser Game Prototype template. Our project directory structure follows the **Phaser Game Prototype Workbook**.

Exercise: Download your bonus content *"Phaser III project starter kit"* zipped files.

Exercise: Review what your *Phaser III project starter kit* files can do here.

2.1 Standardized File Structure

The benefits gained by using either Yeoman or **our FREE Game Prototype template** is that all your projects will have a consistent "look and feel" during each project's development — that means faster, quicker game generation and deployments. It becomes a simple matter to generate a game every 30— or even 7—days! **Imagine this: one year from now, you could have 12 to 52 games in the "Apps store".**

NOTE: Business Considerations, Distribution, Pricing, and Marketing are topics covered in *Phaser III Game Prototyping Part III* and *Phaser III Game Design Part I*.

Complete Single-Player Game File Structure

```
1    ./<PROJECT_NAME>/    //game root directory
2    ├── favicon.ico      //game logo
3    ├── index.html       //game front-door entrance
4    ├── license.txt      //game EULA @ your online store
5    ├── manifest.json    //game mobile app
6    ├── package.json     //for Progressive Web Apps
7    ├── purchaseOrd.pdf //how to buy your game
8    ├── ReadMe.md        //game info & contact
9    │
10   ├── assets/          //game unique © resources
11   │   ├── audio/
12   │   ├── images/
13   │   └── spritesheets/
14   │
15   ├── css/             //game content styling
16   │   └── main.css
17   ├── fonts/           //game font styling
18   │   └── fonts.css
19   │
```

```
20      └── js/            //game behaviors
21          ├── lib/       //game external libraries
22          ├── plugins/   //game enhancements
23          ├── prefabs/   //game prefabrication objects
24          ├── states/    //game phase
25          └── utilities/ //game helpers
```

File Descriptions:

- **index.html** — Main game container file, your example game should be viewed from within this page.

- **.htaccess** — The default web server configs are for Apache. For more information, please refer to the Apache Server Configs documentation. Host your site on a server other than Apache? You're likely to find the corresponding server configs project listed here

- **apple-touch-icon-precomposed.png** — If you want to use different Apple Touch Icons for different resolutions refer to this documentation.

- **crossdomain.xml** — A template for working with cross-domain requests. (*more about crossdomain.xml here*). **WARNING:** WebSockets **can AND do cross-domain communication,** it follows the same cross-origin sharing *CORS methodologies* and **they are not limited** by the "Same Origin Policy (SOP)", as JavaScript is traditionally inside the browser. Because of this, WebSockets have the same exposure to the types of cross-domain attacks. I won't go into detailed descriptions on WebSocket security, simply said, it's up to the server authentication to validate their client's origin and for WebSocket frame tampering. If you'd like to restrict browsers' communication to same-domain servers, you will modify the header policies in the browser Content-Security-Policy header. This will lock down the WebSocket to your originating domain. Naturally, you should always use "wss://" (Secure WebSockets), to ensure a stronger level of encryption.

- **favicon.ico** — refer to Hans's handy HTML5 Boilerplate Favicon and Apple Touch Icon PSD-Template.
- **human.txt** — Edit this file to include the team that worked on your site/app, and the technology powering it.
- **license.txt** — describe how you permit the use of your game.
- **purchaseOrder.pdf** — never know how a consumer obtained your game release; provide them with a means to remain honest.
- **readme.txt** (**FILE_ID.DIZ**, or **readme.md**) should have a customer-friendly welcome, project introduction, installation instructions, license, and contact information.
- **robots.txt** — Edit this file to include any pages you need to be hidden from search engines.
- **assets/** — **Any copyrighted assets (purchased or created) specifically for this game,** or referenced in the index.html file should be in this folder.
  - **audio/** — Home for any audio files. You could simply name this directory "sounds" or "sound effects" (sfx). You might consider building two sub-directories for game theme "music" and another for "sound effects (sfx)". Remember that not all browsers support every audio format (.wav, .ogg, mp3/4). Try creating *your own music here* Research *more demos* from ToneJS — A Web Audio framework for making interactive music in the browser at https://tonejs.github.io. **Learn about the differences between HTML5 audio and Web Audio here.**
  - **data/** — Any data files (e.g. JSON, atlas) that pertain directly utilized by these assets.
  - **fonts/** — Any unique font-sets you have licensed
  - **images/** — Home for any visual files. You could simply name this directory "images", "sprites" or " graphics effects" (gfx). I stuff all the visuals here — including spriteSheets.
  - **maps/** — the information about tile-maps used in this game.
  - **misc./** — any additional files such as dialogs, run-time scripts, language XML/json, etc.

- **data/** — configurations, static data templates, tile maps, game board dimensions, etc.
- **docs/** — This directory contains all the HTML5 Boilerplate documentation and might contain any extra documentation about the Blueprint. You can use it as the location and basis for your own project's documentation.
- **js/** — Source JavaScript files for your game. You could simply name this directory "js" (as I do), "scripts" or *"source (src as other develops do here)".* You could include Libraries, plugins, and custom code; or all can be included in a separate sub-directory or directory. It includes some initial JS to help get you started
  - **gameObjects/** — Any core Game Objects (such as player.js, avatar.js, treasure.js, etc.) should be contained here.
  - **states/** — All Game Phases (aka state, scene, or screen) menus used by your game.
  - **utils/** — Folder containing any Utility Methods/Objects.
  - **game.js (or main.js)** — This is written in **PURE** JavaScript, and manages all the **Game Mechanics (GM)** rules, logic and data structures as a separate file.
- **lib/** — External Libraries that are required/used should be contained here. This includes any JavaScript Framework and addons / extensions (a.k.a., **Plugins**).
  - **phaser.min.js** or simply use from one of the content delivery networks. I strongly recommend against stylized Phaser compilations exclusively for your game release. The current Phaser v3 (minimized) is nearing 1Mb. The chances your gamer has already played a Phaser Game is extremely likely ... meaning Phaser is already in their browser cache. Your exclusive edition is NOT, so you've just added an unnecessary \~ 1Mb to your game's download.
  - **plugins/** — Any Plugins that are used.
- **themes/** — Folder containing any formatting for the overall hosting website.

- **CSS/** — cascading styles sheets for the overall website theme. It should follow a *"structured approach"* creating separate cascading style sheets during development. Upon deployment, all of these collapse into a single file. This directory should contain all your project's CSS files. It includes some initial CSS to help get you started from a solid foundation.
- **gfx/** — graphics effects for the hosting website.

2.2 Barebones Set-up

At a minimum, we only need two files and two directory folders to start our game project:

- An *"index.html"* file that launches your game,
- A "Main.js" file — name it anything you'd like; some folks simply call it "launch.js", "index.js" or "game.js". It's your decision; but once you've decided, please stay consistent! — placed inside the newly created JavaScript ("js") directory folder; and then
- An *"assets directory"* folder in which we'll store all our *game graphics*, sounds, sprites, tilemaps, and images. I call these "game assets" since I've either created or purchased them; they **are the visual copyright-able content**[1]. Let's not worry about putting anything into the "asset directory folders" for now. We'll do that later — after we have our source code drafted and operational.

2.3 Web Server Required - Batteries not included!

One last step for our project set-up is getting our `"index.html"` page to work properly. There are several ways to do this. If you already have *XAMPP* (*WAMP*, or *LAMPP*) installed per *Phaser.io's recommendations*, then we're good to go (and better off than my next suggestion). **If not?** Well, I recommend using the *Brackets editor* tentatively until you know where you'll host your publically accessed game(s). it magically runs those required web services for you.

You should set-up your development workstation **to mimic** your **live web server. Avoid** any Internet Service Provider (ISP) who will not let you work unrestrictedly on your back-end environment. You should have "File Transfer" (*FTP*) and upload privileges for various *back-end software* at a minimum. *Here's an example* of what you should have as a minimum.

Exercise: Explore what a back-end web server *should provide here.*

Another temporary solution I discovered is **Google's Chrome Web server.** Once you install this application, you can launch web pages directly from Chrome. Simply point this application to your project folder.

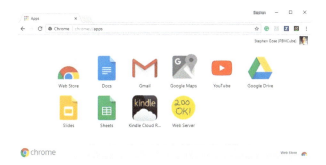

Google Chrome Webserver

OR,

If you're a "C/C++" programmer, I sure you'll enjoy *MiniWeb* — (*source available here*) — a "mini" HTTP server daemon written in C language that is ***embeddable*** in other applications (as a static or dynamic library) as well as a standalone web server. MiniWeb supports transparent 7-zip decompression. MiniWeb can also be used in audio/video streaming applications, or more specifically, VOD (video-on-demand) service. Currently, a VOD client/server is being developed on MiniWeb.

3 Starting a Game Project

We going to jump directly into the "Play Phase" of our game development. This drops us into a **"WHAM!** you're playing now" mode. Later in this tutorial, we'll surround our game loop with a proper "game shell" (aka Content Management System or CMS) illustrated below.

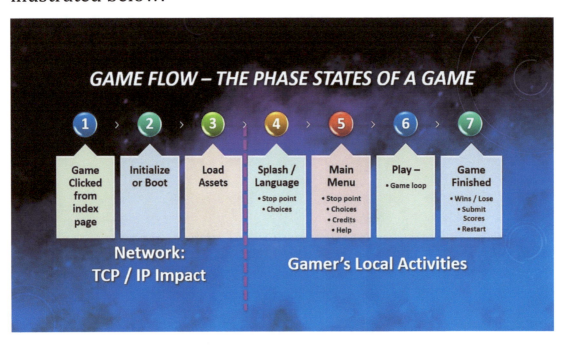

Overall Game Phase Flow in the Game shell

Did you find the words **"Stop Point"** in the illustration? These are excellent points in the game flow to load additional game assets and resources while the gamer is making choices. It's a perfect time *to turn on WebSockets and download more game assets in the background.* (See Appendix: "How to Start a WebSocket")

WebSocket is thoroughly discussed in "Making Massive Multi-Player Online Games".

There are "8 Steps" in the Game Recipe™ process and they are explained fully in *"Phaser Game Design Workbook"* pages 63-65. We'll follow those recommended steps while we create this project.

3.1 Step 0: Review your competition and their games

This is the fun part when developing a new game — so, enjoy! (*Boy and Girl Scouts: Earn your Merit Badge!*)

- Research, find and play similar gaming genres, currently on the market, that match your ideas and appeal to similar target audiences.
- Record which websites host this game genre and
- Investigate their submission policies.
- Record what game features your competitors have in their games. (This is also the first step of 8 for "Game Deployment" covered more thoroughly in *Phaser Game Prototyping.)*
- Make a list of the minimum features you initially want. This becomes your encoding task list.

Game Examples

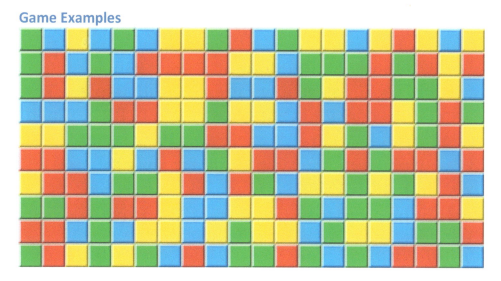

SameGame or Collapsing Blocks gameplay

This *"Game Recipe"™* offers several unique demonstrations:

- ***NCC Pandora** (demo here)* — and transpiled from our 1996 released BBS game. Collapsing Block puzzle games are very interesting in themselves. The secret is mixing the Collapsing Block puzzle into a story and integrating it with other game mechanics.

- Simple demonstration at
  https://www.mindgames.com/game/SameGame — with license protection notes. Study *embedded protection*.
- Similar game mechanics *found on Phaser.io*.
- Pure *HTML5 Table* implementation.

3.2 Step 1: Create your "front-door"

We'll begin working on our game's front door — the *"index.html"* file. Create or download it from the supporting website. ***Notice you do not need to change any of its content (except for the metadata)!*** This is because we've created this initial "front door into our game" in a standardized generic format that applies to any game creation within this series. Software engineers call this ***D.R.Y. (Don't Repeat Yourself)*** coding; it saves your time by creating things once and re-using them; it's a *"building block style"* (similar to children's blocks created by the Lego Company) or **black-box development**.

Choose whether we are creating a standard or mobile game. Using *"responsive design"* only addresses how the game will display on any device. There are other considerations such as CPU, RAM, Cloud Services, and "off-line" web-workers. Then, if you chose a mobile game, you should determine whether you want a mobile *"single web page application" (SWPA)* or *Progressive Web App (PWA)* or perhaps just stick with the more traditional HTML5 structure.

A *"single web page application" (SWPA)* contains everything inside its *"index.html"* page as a "stand-alone" delivery. The *"game.js"* for the "Play Phase" becomes either a script tag loading an external file or you might consider embedding your entire JS code inside the *"<script>"* tag. This will determine where the *"Main.js"* will reside which holds all the game rules, logic, and data structures — as an external module or entirely embedded inside the *"index.html"* page.

Exercise: Create the following "index.html" file.

Bare Bones index.html - 'the Game's Front Door'

```html
 1    <!DOCTYPE html>
 2    <html lang="en">
 3        <head>
 4            <meta charset="utf-8" />
 5            <meta http-equiv="X-UA-Compatible" content="IE=Edge;chrome=1">
 6            <title> (Your Game title) </title>
 7
 8    <!-- CSS styles always precedes any JS scripts -->
 9            <style type = "text/css">
10                body{
11                    background: #000000;
12                    padding: 0px;
13                    margin: 0px;
14                }
15                canvas{
16                    display:block;
17                    margin: 0;
18                    position: absolute;
19                    top: 50%;
20                    left: 50%;
21                    transform: translate(-50%, -50%);
22                }
23            </style>
24
25    <!-- for faster load times always use a CDN  -->
26    <script src="https://cdn.jsdelivr.net/npm/phaser@3.24.1/dist/phaser.js">
27    </script>
28
29    <!-- Phaser Gaming Framework always precedes any game scripts -->
30    <!-- REMEMBER Phaser v2 IS NOT COMPATIBLE WITH PHASER v3 -->
31    <!-- ///////////////////////////////////////////////////
32    NOTE: Phaser library must be loaded before any game logic.
33    We load script files here to avoid windows.onload call.
34    Window.onload is rarely used for many reasons, and because
35    Phaser doesn't wait until all resources are loaded.
36    The DOMContentLoaded event triggers when the page is ready.
37    It waits only for the full HTML and scripts to load then starts.
38    This is explained in greater detail in
39    "Phaser.Js Design Guide workbook".
40    https://leanpub.com/phaser3gamedesignworkbook/.
41
42    NOTE: per the "Phaser.JS Design Guide",
43      you may place the following script externally or
44      as the last head script using defer.
45    ///////////////////////////////////////////////////
46
47     TODO:
48        - Game Development using multiple files
49        to find bugs easily.
```

```
50        - in live deployment always use defer
51    ////////////////////////////////////////////////
52        <script defer src="js/boot.js"></script>
53        <script defer src="js/load.js"></script>
54        <script defer src="js/menu.js"></script>
55        <script defer src="js/play.js"></script>
56        <script defer src="js/game.js"></script>
57    -->
58        </head>
59
60        <body>
61            <div id="gameDiv"> (game canvas is here) </div>
62        </body>
63
64    </html>
```

Reminder: If you are using a modern browser (roughly anything since 2018), you could use "modules" in your gaming projects **(without needing to use Webpack2, Parcel, and such tools)** by adding the `type="module"` attribute into the HTML5 script tag. This topic is fully discussed in ***Phaser Game Prototyping Workbook.***

<script ***type="module"*** defer src="./js/play.js" > </script>

Build a responsive web page in 15 seconds at http://www.initializr.com/.

Excellent work! Our game page's "front door" is ready to use and boot-up our game. Creating our game mechanics source code is our next step; let's move on to Step 2.

3.3 Step 2. Create your "Game Shell" & Phases

The Game Shell and Logic Flow of HTML5 Games.

Let's take a "10,000-foot" review of the **game shell, game architecture, game phases, and encoding formats** before we begin constructing our core game.

The HTML5 Game "logical flow" is the path your gamers use **despite which Phaser JavaScript Framework version you're using.** It is our game's "architecture". When a gamer launches your game from its *"index.html"* page, we lead them through a series of **game phases**

(aka "menu screens" similar to Adobe Flash Games). Some developers call these "game states" — which is the proper technical terminology about the Finite State Machine (FSM). Eventually, our gamers will arrive and click a "play" button somewhere on the "main menu" to start the "Gaming Loop".

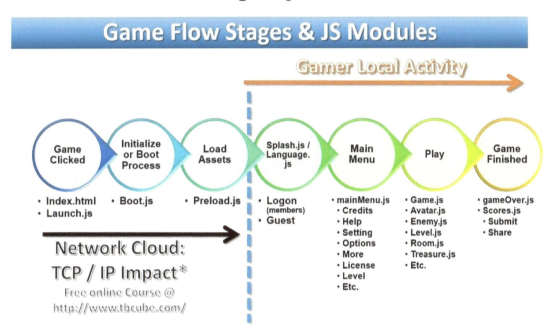

All Games follow these Phases & Logic Flow

The former "game state" (aka "life-cycles") in Phaser v2.x.x are now called **"scenes"** in Phaser v3.4+ and are managed quite differently than the former v2.x.x. *Don't confuse these "Game Phases" with Phaser's terminology.*

Here's another *game programming flow chart* located in your bonus content or from here: https://makingbrowsergames.com/starterkits/_GameFlowChart.pdf. It demonstrates the same concepts illustrated above. Notice it has *nothing to do with which Phaser version you're using! This applies to ANY Gaming Framework you may implement!*

We'll create all these supporting "game phases" as separate JavaScript (JS) files later in this tutorial.[1] When we create them, we'll place these files inside either the "`/js/states/`" directory or "`/js/state-as-classes/`" directory depending on your JS syntax.

- `Play.js` — which *IS our game's loop* and the majority of the work found in this chapter.

Progressive Rendering

Optimizing for performance is all about understanding what happens in these intermediate steps between receiving the HTML, CSS, and JavaScript bytes and the required processing to turn them into rendered pixels - that's the critical rendering path.

By optimizing the critical rendering path we can significantly improve the time to the first rendering of our pages. Further, understanding the critical rendering path also serves as a foundation for building well-performing interactive applications. The interactive updates process is the same, just done in a continuous loop and ideally at 60 frames per second! But first, an overview of how the browser displays a simple page.

You will learn how to optimize any website for speed by diving into the details of how mobile and desktop browsers render pages. You'll learn about the Critical Rendering Path, or the set of steps browsers must take to convert HTML, CSS, and JavaScript into a living, breathing website. From there, you'll start exploring and experimenting with tools to measure performance and simple strategies to deliver the first pixels to the screen as early as possible. You'll learn how to dive into recommendations from PageSpeed Insights and the Timeline view of Google Chrome's Developer Tools to find the data you need to achieve immediate performance boosts!

This is a **FREE** course offered through *Udacity*.

Network Impact

Placing your game as close to your players as possible will help their perception of how quick and lively your game is. "How do we ensure our game deployment is close to our consumers?", you say? By **using a content delivery network (CDN)!** The sample `"index.html"` source code offers two choices when downloading the Phaser Game Framework from a content delivery network. Once your game reaches the "splash/language" phase, all activity then occurs on the gamer's device as a "single-player" game.

Let's review those next three-game phases `"boot"`, `"preload"`, **and** `"splash"` after the network delivers the game's `"index.html"` page. Normally, your gamers would see a progress bar then after a few seconds, the first "splash" or "language selection" menu appears. The network has the most impact on our game during these initial three phases.

Gamer's Local Activity

Let's review those game phases which compose the "game's shell". We'll create all of them once we have our game working. Since each phase in our game shell performs similar tasks using the ***"Phaser Essential Functions" (aka "life-cycle" discussed next),*** it is easy to keep them ***D.R.Y.*** so, once we write a `game shell` **we're done** — except for small unique modifications or features we may want. When we create new graphics files — but label them with the same names we have in our `game shell` — we are simply replacing the previous game art with new art (by using the same file names; we are ***intentionally overwriting*** them), and **VOILA! NEW GAME** ... same game mechanics, same source code, yet with different "look & feel" artwork — ***this is the secret sauce for cranking out a game per week.***

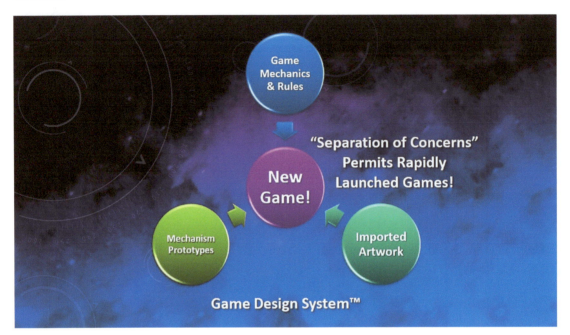

Phaser III Game Design Workbook

D.R.Y. Speed Limit - 5 GPH (Games Per Hour)!

Quoted from ***"Phaser III Game Starter Kit Collection", page 245.***

"Now, take this simple example to the next level of complexity! **Exchange** all the fox silhouettes and the background image but keep your modified code (as above) **D.R.Y. Voila!** new game ... how long did that take? You're just uploading new artwork! You should have merely changed the new artwork to the same file names you already had in this project. **YEAP!** overwriting the old art with completely new files. ***Let's pretend it took 55 minutes to find 5 new theme backgrounds and silhouettes; and then in the next 5 minutes, you created 5 different games.*** That's the power the ***Game Design System™*** offers you."

The only "game phases" we need to visit and *tweak* are the:

- *main.js (as delegation theory):* holds all the particular configurations, the data structure(s), and supporting functions of our ***game's mechanics, rules, and logic.*** However, should we build similar game products, this file could be relatively ***D.R.Y.*** By keeping the *"`main.js`" (i.e., **"game mechanics component, rules, and logic")** and exchanging either (or both) the "game mechanisms component" (i.e., those visual elements, head-up displays, and User Interfaces) or "artwork component" (i.e., game aesthetic), we have created a new game product!

- *boot.js (or classful version):* it lists all the game assets needed initially. If we standardized and maintain our "file naming conventions", we simply have to create new artwork with the **same file names** found in the *"`boot.js`"* file and add any new artwork items for this specific game edition. In short, we simply exchanged the game aesthetic used by the game mechanisms; this changes the "look and feel" without changing the mechanics nor mechanisms.

- *splash or language.js (or classful version):* the more standardized this menu is the better. The encoding required is the new language text's content assigned to its specific text variable. Changing languages will update the text variable content (containers holding the language expressions) with the gamer's language choice.

- *menu.js (or classful version):* Perhaps, we might perform small tweaks to our menu for unique options for a specific game(?); however, the more standardized this main menu is the better. The main menu should provide gamers with business supporting information and a button to launch the game's "play phase" (i.e., "game loop"). Finally,

- *play.js (or classful version):* which **IS our game's loop** and the majority of the work found **in this tutorial.** This file launches the game core mechanisms and supporting functions. This is the only file that should be tailored. YET, when using the **Game Design system™** with its **Game Recipes™ and tools,** this becomes a simple matter of `importing/including` fresh "Game Mechanics".

Each of these game phases is governed internally by the same "Essential Phaser functions ("life-cycle")" *(see "Inside each Phase" discussed later)*. Each Game Phase is responsible for its own internal "Phaser Essential Functions" and control.

ES5 Format

Your game's "architecture" — expressed as "game phases" — could be written in an older ES5 format — tools such as *Babel convert* (aka a *"transcompile"*) your JS code back into ES5 format. Let's write these game phases into code. Here's what our **Phaser game skeleton framework** looks like.

Exercise: Download and review the older ES5 style: *https://makingbrowsergames.com/starterkits/_gameSkeleton.pdf*

This source code, from the exercise above, is a generic pattern across all my Phaser games. I write it into the **"`game.js`"** (or **"`main.js`"**) to hold all the game mechanics, logic, rules, and data structures written in "Pure" JavaScript; it becomes my "Game Mechanics Component". The files above become our "standard game creation template" *for either Phaser v2.x.x or v3.16+*. I call this my "game skeleton". Phaser is extremely flexible and adds several innovative ways to achieve a similar "game set-up".

With your file you downloaded from the exercise, let's quickly review its content.

- Line 1, we should "`use strict`" to avoid fat-fingering, nasty bugs, poor assignments, and the like.
- Line 2, Comments are our friends. Use them generously!

- Line 3, Console logging is our best friend and worth the investigation to use properly.
- Line 6: Let's declare a "`global application object`" or "namespace". This creates our JavaScript game (object) — a "constructor" as folks in Object-Oriented Programming (OOP) call it — and then inside this object, we set the game's dimensions to the *Golden Ratio*. Our Phaser game will live inside this JavaScript object and is protected from memory collisions. This is the "namespace technique"; our game has various "phases and menus" which our gamer will use to play our game; the namespace will be kept safely in this "`global object`". These suggestions are not the only way to create JavaScript namespaces.
- Line 17: extends our newly created "Game" object with a prototype inheritance chain. This attaches all of our internal game functions to our newly created object above. This is ***not the only*** way to create an internal method of "literals" or "lambdas". Modifying any root "Object" prototype — such as array — ***is a particularly bad anti-pattern*** according to this established and highly respected JavaScript reference. *"Learning JavaScript Design Patterns"* — Read this **FREE book.**
- Lines 18 to 22: are the Phaser Essential Functions (aka the "life-cycle" for either API version) and for any of our "game phases". Later, we'll learn some interesting secrets about Phaser III.
- Line 19: "`preloads`" game assets. Remember the game must be active within 20 seconds or we stand rejection from "app stores".
- Line 20: "`create`" ties our newly downloaded assets into the game's display list.
- Line 21: "`update`" will continually read the inputs and modifications then display (aka "render") those results for our gamers.
- Line 22: "`render`" is reserved for new information after the displayed updates and is the typical location for debug information.

- Line 28 to 34: Ties the Phaser v2.x.x Game Engine and framework into a variable for our DOM canvas tag.
- Line 36 to 47: is a glimpse into what's new in Phaser III — to quote Dorothy from the Wizard of Oz, **"We're not in Kansas anymore!"** Remember, Phaser v2.x.x API IS NOT COMPATIBLE WITH PHASER v3.

ES6+ Format as *"FAT Arrow"* Function

Your game's "architecture", as "game phases", could be written in the common ES6+ format in several ways. Three ES6+ versions of the "game skeleton" are provided below.

ES6 as *FAT Arrow* Functions

```
1    var config = {
2        type: Phaser.AUTO,
3        width: 800,
4        height: 500,
5        physics: {
6            default: 'arcade',
7            arcade: {
8                gravity: {y: 500},
9                debug: true
10           }
11       },
12       scene: {
13           key: 'play',
14           preload: preload,
15           create: create,
16           update: update
17       }
18   };
19
20   var game = new Phaser.Game(config);
21
22   var map;
23   var player;
24   var cursors;
25   var groundLayer, coinLayer;
26   var text;
27
28   var preload = () => { ... }
29
30   var create = () => { ... }
```

```
31
32      var update = () => { ... }
```

ES6 introduced a new way of writing concise function statements; they are called "FAT Arrow" functions. It is important to understand the difference between "normal" functions and "FAT Arrow" functions because they behave differently. "FAT Arrow" functions are anonymous; they are not named. This poses a problem when debugging and the self-referencing *"this"* is *lexically* bound. What that means is *"this"* refers to the code that contains the arrow function.

"FAT Arrow" functions do ***not*** replace "normal functions". There is a time and place to use the "FAT Arrow" style correctly. The best circumstances to use "FAT Arrow" functions is when anything that requires *"this"* to be bound to the context, and not a function itself. Never use "FAT Arrow" functions as:

- ***Object methods.*** ES6 'Fat Arrow Functions' **were never intended to become an internal "Class" method.** *Quoted from MDN*, "arrow function expressions ***are best suited for non-method functions."***
- Callback functions ***with dynamic content.***
- When it makes your source code "less" readable.

Deeper Dive: Using "FAT Arrow" functions. Review the following articles.

- *ES5 functions vs. ES6 'fat arrow' functions*
- *"When (and why) you should use ES6 arrow functions — and when you shouldn't"*
- *Arrow Function vs Function in JS*

ES6+ Format as *"Phaser.Class"*

ES6 style object literal - using Phaser.Class

```
1      // This is NOT an ES6 example
2      // TODO: Find and refactor variables in the "<...>".
3      // https://github.com/photonstorm/phaser/blob/v3.22.0/src/utils/Class.
```

```js
 4
 5      /**
 6       * NOTE: the alternate acceptable form for ES6 and TypeScript
 7       * Classes are NOT hoisted.
 8       *
 9       * Alternate syntax per
10       * "Professional JavaScript for Web Developers 3rd Edition" pg: 873
11       * class <Phaser_State_Name> prototype Phaser.Scene {
12       */
13
14      // method #1: using object literal
15      var <GamePhaseName> = new Phaser.Class({
16
17          Extends: Phaser.Scene,
18
19          initialize: function <GamePhaseName> (config) {
20              Phaser.Scene.call(this, { key: '<GamePhaseName>',config });
21          },
22
23          preload: function preload () {
24              this.load.image(
25                      '<GamePhaseNameBackGround>',
26                      'assets/images/<GamePhaseName>.png'
27              );
28          },
29
30          create: function create (data) {
31              this.add.image(0, 0,
32                  '<GamePhaseNameBackGround>').setOrigin(0);
33              this.input.once('pointerdown', function () {
34                  console.log('From <GamePhaseName> to <NextPhaseName>');
35                  this.scene.start('<NextPhaseName>');
36              }, this);
37          },
38
39          update: function (time, delta) {}
40
41      });
```

Architecture Consideration: Using the example above locks us into the Phaser Gaming Framework. It's worth noting that this "class" sets up a pattern that we'll use again in future projects. The <GamePhaseName>.js exports a class that requires Phaser.Class and extends Phaser.Scene. I've seen other developers use the same concepts to even extend Phaser.GameObjects.Sprite. Instead, you should start embracing a *more flexible component pattern.* For example, where a Player's avatar has a "data property" reference rather than a Player's avatar binding directly into `Phaser.GameObjects.Sprite`.

MDN says, "An important difference between function declarations and class declarations is that **function declarations are hoisted** and class declarations are **not.** You first need to declare your class and then access it, otherwise, code like the following will throw a `ReferenceError`".

ES6+ Format as _"Phaser.Scene"_

Game Phases for any JS Gaming Framework.

Don't confuse my description of "Game Phases" with Phaser's "Scene" terminology. You can run multiple "`Phaser.Scene`" inside a single "Game Phase". A "`Phaser.Scene`" can only run one physics engine — either "Arcade", "Impact", or "MatterJS" — unlike Phaser v2.x.x. See this Phaser v3.16+ example for running *"Multiple Physics"*.

traditional ES6 style object literal

```
1    /**
2     * NOTE: the alternate acceptable form for ES6 and TypeScript
3     * Classes are NOT hoisted.
4     *
5     * Alternate syntax per
6     * "Professional JavaScript for Web Developers 3rd Edition" pg: 873
7     * class <Phaser_State_Name> prototype Phaser.Scene {
8     */
9
10   // method #2: using object literal
11   class <GamePhaseName> extends Phaser.Scene {
12     constructor() {
13       super('<GamePhaseName>');
14     },
15
16       preload() {
17         // load images
18         this.load.image(
19               '<GamePhaseNameBackGround>',
```

```
20                  'assets/images/<GamePhaseName>.png'
21              );
22          },
23
24          create: function create (data) {
25              this.add.image(0, 0,
26                  '<GamePhaseNameBackGround>').setOrigin(0);
27              this.input.once('pointerdown', function () {
28                  console.log('From <GamePhaseName> to <NextPhaseName>');
29                  this.scene.start('<NextPhaseName>');
30              }, this);
31          },
32
33          update: function (time, delta) {}
34      }
```

Now that we have an idea about the game shell, game architecture, game phases, and encoding formats. Let's set all of these aside for now and just focus on building a working game prototype.

Part II: Making *"Collapsing Blocks"* Browser Games

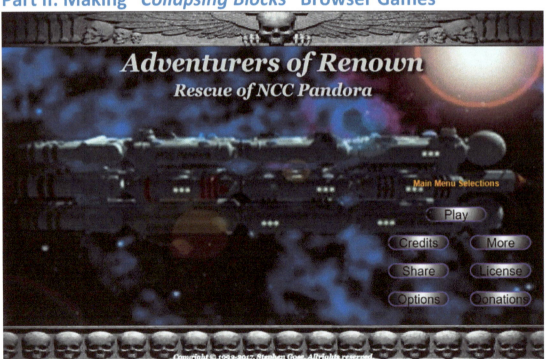

Sample Main Menu

A starter Kit for Collapsing Blocks Game Mechanics

Web-Master Game License for the single-player version included below — use these licenses to quickly deploy this game on your website.

- General **non-exclusive license.**
- registered to affiliate: **PBMCube.com** (see the *affiliate guide*).
- Phaser III General License: **54c73155-3555-4f5c-a19c-3e6eb4478f42**

See the *"End-User License Agreement" (EULA)* here. Please register *your book here* or at my *email contact*.

4 Collapsing Blocks — Core Game Construction

4.1 Game Project Overview

The **Collapsing Blocks** Game Starter Kit is an easy-to-use blueprint for any of the Phaser.js JavaScript Gaming Framework API (v2.x.x, CE, or v3.16+); it has all the game mechanisms and logic that you need for a complete **Collapsing Blocks game.** Phaser is among the top open-source HTML5 / JavaScript game development frameworks. It is certainly a powerful tool when combined with GUI-editors and the former Cocoon (defunct as of 4 FEB 2019)[1]. Phaser liberates your design decisions since it is "pure" JavaScript. It offers complete freedom over your game design patterns, artwork selections, and your chosen deployment venues. I have been using **Phaser Game Framework** for quite some time now; and, have created this series of **Game Recipes™** (aka "Game Starter Kit" or "Blue Prints") which you might find beneficial in launching your own game projects. Furthermore, I created other game development tools to help me generate new game ideas, create game design documentation (GDD), technical design documentation (TDD), and foundation source code.

Visit
https://makingbrowsergames.com/gameDesigner/
and try them yourself.

4.2 Our Goal

I would like to guide you in creating responsive delivery styles for **Collapsing Blocks** games — for either mobile devices or standard browsers. We will use these game mechanics, mechanisms, and the development methods discussed in the references above. By the end of this chapter, you should have a fully functional **Collapsing Blocks** game using your own bespoke gaming assets.

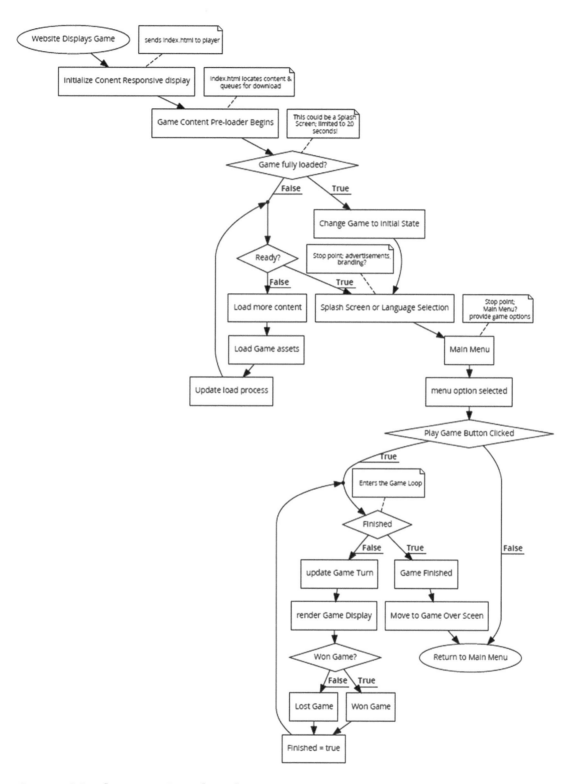

Game Mechanics Single-Player Core

4.3 Collapsing Blocks Genre Description

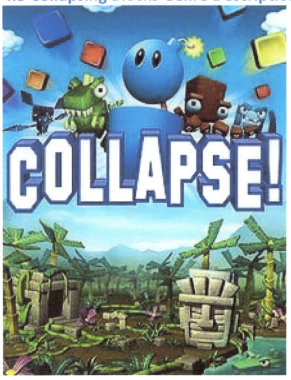

COLLAPSE! promotional screen art

The **Collapsing Blocks mechanics** was a series of award-winning "tile-matching, puzzle, video games" by the popular *GameHouse Company*. It was first released in 1998 under the title of "Collapse!" The series was discontinued in 2015 due to the closure of the *"RealNetworks" game studio*. My observation from hundreds of arcade sites concludes that Collapsing Blocks is still a popular game with a better than average rating. Originally, the grandfather of this game mechanics comes from "SameGame" (さめがめ) is a *tile-matching* puzzle originally released under the name *Chain Shot!* in 1985 by Kuniaki Moribe (Morisuke). It has since been ported to numerous computer platforms and hand-held devices, with its newest versions released in 2016.

Tile-matching video game

Quote: "The core challenge of "tile-matching games" is the identification of patterns on a seemingly chaotic board. Their origins lie in late 1980s games such as *Tetris*, *Chain Shot!* (SameGame) and *Puzznic*. Tile-matching games were made popular in the 2000s, in the form of casual games distributed or played over the Internet, notably the Bejeweled series of games.[3] They have remained popular since, with the game Candy Crush Saga becoming the most-played game on Facebook in 2013.[4][5]"

"Tile-matching games cover a broad range of design elements, mechanics, and gameplay experiences. They include purely turn-based games but may also feature arcade-style action elements such as time pressure, shooting, or hand-eye coordination. The tile-matching mechanic is also a minor feature in some larger games. Video game researcher Jesper Juul, therefore, considers tile matching to be a game mechanic, rather than a distinct genre of games.[6]"

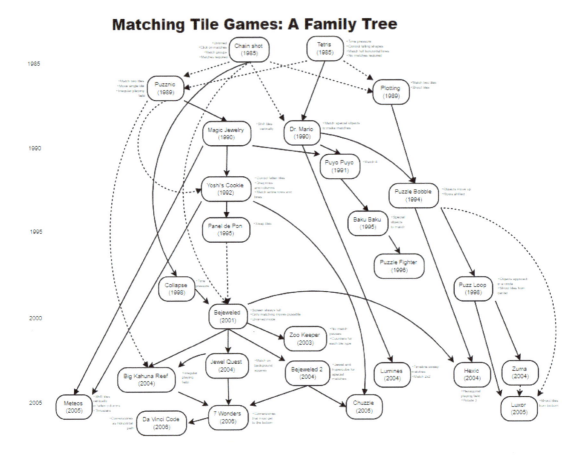

Beginnings of Collapsing Blocks Game Mechanics

Exercise: Read this detailed analysis and game design issues on the *family development tree* for "matching games" from
Exercise: Read the *historical development of "Chain-Shot"* and the *variation created*.
Exercise: Read the code for this *Highly Optimized version of SameGame (1kB!)* which is perfect for mobile deployments.

4.4 Game Mechanics (GM): Logic & Rules

The classic Collapsing Blocks game is played on a large game board grid — software implementation is typically a 2D array of 12 columns by 15 rows. Various randomly colored blocks — typically 4 to 7 different colors as images or simple graphics — fill the game area. There is only one rule and objective to this game — click groups of two or more adjacent blocks of the same type or color. That selected group is removed from the game, points are earned by the group size eliminated. Replacement blocks fill in the vacated spaces of the game area — generally, from the top. See **more scoring options** from Wikipedia. The larger the group of connected and adjacent matching colors the higher the score earned.

Several variations on the game's mechanics replenish the play area from different sides. The objective remains the same — to delete groups of similar cells and prevent the game area from completely filling up and reaching the top row or beyond. *Other variations* include "special blocks" that would contribute more points or that would delete rows or columns regardless of colors contained. Others use hexagonal grids instead of squares or pearls. Additional variations allow for limited rotations of the gameboard area, special privileges, or restricted game-time per difficulty level. Review the variety of *rules and variations here*.

4.5 Game Mechanics (GM): Data Structure

The primary method to determine groups of blocks is called "Flood fill or seed fill". It is similar in concept to a "bucket fill tool" in graphical painting applications. The flood-fill function takes three variables: a starting position, a selected color, and its replacement color. Our source code searches for all positions adjacent to that selected piece with the same color and simply records or places them into a queue for further processing. The common data structure chosen is through queues or stacks to manage these collected pieces. Wikipedia provides several methods to search and choose pieces in either a four-way or eight-way validation.

- Stack-based recursive implementation (four-way)
- Forest Fire algorithm (queuing method)
- Fixed-memory method (right-hand fill) — the method I choose to present in this tutorial.

The "Fixed-memory method" uses practically nothing in RAM for those four adjacent positions; this is a critical consideration for mobile devices. The game's source code pretends to paint the game area without boxing itself into a corner.[2] Our game source code could discover itself then in several states:

1. All four boundary pixels are filled.
2. Three of the boundary pixels are filled.
3. Two of the boundary pixels are filled.
4. One boundary pixel is filled.
5. Zero boundary pixels are filled.

4.6 Game Recipe™ Featured Ingredients

Our Collapsing Blocks Game (aka "Tile-matching" or "SameGame") typically has the following mechanisms and game mechanics:

- Short play sessions. *Quote:* "In a survey on the Trymedia web site, 66% of players reported that their typical play session lasts more than an hour (Macrovision 2006). The key is that casual games allow short play sessions, hence making it easier for players to commit to playing a game."
- Tilemap Creation for the play area grid (unique to gaming framework used).
- The recursive logic for match selection, validation, and removal (common game mechanics).
- User Interface (UI) on the Tile — i.e., click/hit detection (unique to gaming framework used).
- Timers and delay events (unique to gaming framework used).
- Arcade physics (unique to gaming framework used).
- Game-board grid as typical squares or possible hexagonal layouts (construction common game mechanics; the display is unique to gaming framework used).
- Scoring, awards, hints, and other "positive informational text" displays in the gamer's native language (common JS game component and the display are unique to the gaming framework used).

- Artificial Intelligence (AI) assistant that tutors oversights, or hard-to-find matches, or as an antagonist second player.
- Moderate innovation — per Jesper Juul[3], "It must be very easy to learn to play casual games. This tends to mean that casual games are near clones of an existing game with new graphics, or that innovation happens in small incremental steps. Steve Meretzky says that it should be possible to state the rules of a casual game in three sentences." (Barwood & Falstein 2006, #107)

If you take this list and login to my *"game design tools"* and enter the information above, my website will generate a "game design document" (GDD), a "technical design document" (TDD), and a foundation source code as a prototype.

4.7 Design Considerations

Collapsing Blocks games are just a simple "tile-matching" puzzle; how can one create an interesting game from such simplistic game mechanics? The answer is **composite construction** — combining *Collapsing Block* with a background story and ***other engaging gameplay mechanics.***

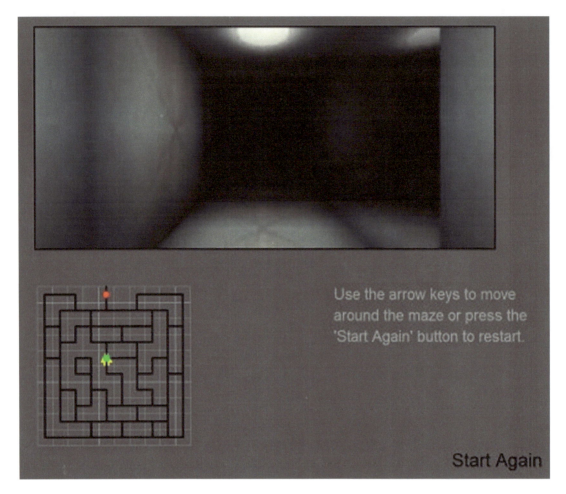

Initial NCC Pandora Flash (SWF) 1st Person prototype – searching for the Computer Terminals

- What is the motivating story to play the game?
- What is "matched"? Colors, numbers, letters, icons, emojis, flowers, shapes, ad nauseam …?
- How many? The more "tiles" types raise the difficulty level; the fewer similar tiles create an easier level.
- What is the Game's objective? to empty the playing field?
- What are the Grid's Size and cell's shapes? Nearly everyone uses squares, but what if you used triangles or hexagons (6-sided flood-fill) or "circles" (8-sided flood-fills)?

The purpose of this "game phase" file is to launch and set-up the "Game Loop". So, let's dive straight into creating the game board area, entities, and pieces. As you have seen, separating our code into these various files is a very good practice during the initial development stages of our game project. Other than the small "mental" memory footprint this provides during software project management, it also gives us more focus on those immediate game actions and logic driving our game while we prototype. More importantly, we can re-use our *"black-box source code"* as a "cookie-cutter" and *"stamp"* more games of the same genre!

Exercise: Review a *generic version of the "play.js" file* here or a **classful version (method 1) here**. This tutorial uses this template to build our "play" game phase. Review the demonstration games this tutorial provides and open your browser console to watch how the Phaser Game Framework interacts.

https://makingbrowsergames.com/starterkits/collapsingblocks /

Exercise: Read about *"Stampit API"* — Creating objects from *standardized*, reusable, composable behaviors. ***Stampit*** is a 1.3KB gzipped (or 2.7K minified) JavaScript module which supports three different kinds of "Prototypal Inheritance" (delegation, concatenation, and functional) to let you inherit behavior in a way that is much **more powerful and flexible** than any other "Object-Oriented Programming" (OOP) model.

Since this game genre's code has a small amount of code managing its logic and rules from the **Game Mechanics Component**, I sometimes consolidate the "Play Phase" and its **Game Mechanisms Component** into a single *"main.js" file.* **"Why?", you ask?** Because all those game mechanics functions were already loaded and ready when the gamer is ready to move into the "play" phase.

4.9 Step 3b: Create Supporting functions.

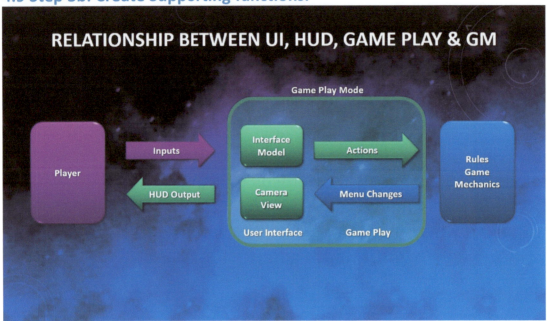

Game Design System™

The following functions support the ***Collapsing Blocks*** game logic and handle "user interactions" (UI), heads-up display (HUD), and "view models". I have included them in our practice game project's "`main.js`" to merge and minimize the number of files downloaded. I have used simple structural programming which is typical for JavaScript, but have grouped functions so that they might become **ES6 "class frosting". (See footnote** [4]**)**

There is sugar for **faking classes** coming to JavaScript (I strongly discourage using it). What would it look like if we created sugar for "Prototypal OO" that supported all of the best features JavaScript has to offer? The result of that exploration was (as far as I know) the most popular prototype-based inheritance library for JavaScript: *Stampit*.

4.10 Conclusion

We are equipped with sufficient information to begin our "encoding phase". It's time to choose which Phaser Gaming Framework you'd like to use — Phaser v2.x.x. or Phaser III.

5 Phaser v3.16+ Code Review

The following functions support the **Collapsing Blocks** game logic, rules, and manage user interactions. This component will "chat" with your selected "JS Gaming Framework". The mechanisms component comes from your "JS Gaming Framework" implementation and will handle the devices' display and User Interfaces (UI). The "artwork component" will supply the graphics and multimedia for the "mechanism prototypes". The "game mechanics and rules" I have included in the "game.js" to merge and minimize the number of files downloaded. I have used simple structural programming which is typical for JavaScript, but I have grouped functions into their ES6 "class frosting".

5.1 Game Set-up Options — Lines 555 to 643

Refer to https://makingbrowsergames.com/starterkits/collapsingblocks/v3.x.x/game.js. This function prepares the game configurations for Phaser III. It cycles through each row and column and assigns a random tile. There are dozens of parameters available.
(See: https://github.com/photonstorm/phaser/blob/master/src/core/Config.js)

- Line 559 creates the "game" object namespace.
- Lines 561 to 597 — is the standard Phaser III configuration object.
- Line 563 uses the `Phaser.AUTO` to dynamically choose either CANVAS or WEBGL.
- Lines 571 to 574 — are specific to your game.
- Lines 575 to 584 — configures the input manager.

- Line 587, 592 — tells Phaser to create a <div> and assigns the ID of "game-area".
- Lines 596 to 606 — would seem to belong inside the Game Mechanisms, but I've chosen to set these aside for an enhancement — to let the user or game developer dynamically select different artwork size, gameboard offsets, and game reaction speeds. I can now expose these in a "Game Settings" menu and let the gamer choose different artwork.
- Lines 609 to 627 — are a "pure JavaScript" method for re-sizing the game within the browser window. Yes, I could achieve the same effect from within the Phaser configurations. (See commented lines 417 to 421) But I decided to demonstrate that you don't need Phaser **to do everything!**
- Lines 479 to the End — is the modern ("acceptable") way to launch games. For more details refer to *Phaser III Game Design* for how to avoid common pitfalls.

"flood fill" Example

The adjacent blocks' discovery has several algorithms *described here*.

flood fill function

```
1      //
2      // =========================================================
3      // flood fill function.
4      _floodFill: function(row,col,val){
5          if(row>=0 && row<GAMEAPP.cellSize && col>=0 && col<GAMEAPP.cellSiz
e){
6              if(gameGrid[row][col]!=null && gameGrid[row][col].frame==val){
7                  gameGrid[row][col].destroy();
8                  GAMEAPP.score += 1;
9                  gameGrid[row][col]=null;
10                 //difficult 4-way search; North, South, West, East
11                 GAMEAPP._floodFill(row+1,col,val);
12                 GAMEAPP._floodFill(row-1,col,val);
13                 GAMEAPP._floodFill(row,col+1,val);
14                 GAMEAPP._floodFill(row,col-1,val);
15                 //easy 8-way search; NE, NW, SE, SW
16                 /*
17                 GAMEAPP._floodFill(row+1,col+1,val);
```

```
18              GAMEAPP._floodFill(row+1,col-1,val);
19              GAMEAPP._floodFill(row-1,col+1,val);
20              GAMEAPP._floodFill(row-1,col-1,val);
21              */
22          } //end if
23      }  //end if
24  },
```

NOTE: You can download this content management system (CMS) file from
https://makingbrowsergames.com/starterkits/collapsingblocks/p3 _collapsingblocks_mainJS.pdf
or the SWPA from
https://makingbrowsergames.com/starterkits/collapsingblock s/v3.x.x/game.js

Review this 8-page file; it is thoroughly annotated and documented to reduce the price of this book.

5.2 Game Mechanisms Component - "playGame" Class

Game Mechanisms relationship to Game Mechanics

The **Game Design System™** separates the Game Mechanics from the Game Mechanisms found in the Phaser III Gaming Framework. The trick is to gather everything concerning Phaser into a "Game

Mechanism Component", and place all the rules and logic into the Game Mechanics Component (as pure JavaScript). When you're ready to move your game into augmented reality (AR) or virtual reality (VR), it becomes a simple matter of replacing Phaser display mechanisms with your 3D support.

So with this in mind — and thoroughly covered in *Phaser III Game Prototyping,* — our game.js has two sections:

- ***PlayGame*** class — Lines 73 to 362.
- ***cBlocksGM*** class — Lines 363 to 613.
- Refer to

https://makingbrowsergames.com/starterkits/collapsingblocks/v3.x.x/game.js.

PlayGame.constructor – Lines 74 to 76

Nothing special here; it's just the normal ES6 class construction.

"Preload" Essential Functions – Lines 80 to 87

Again nothing new here either. The "preload" essential function (unique to Phaser Gaming Framework) loads game assets. You'll notice that I'm could load two different tilesets. One spriteSheet (loaded) only has four tiles and the other has five (see `assets/sprites/compButtons.jpg`). Using a "4-tile spriteSheet" provides easier gameplay and quick matches. We could use this for an "easy or beginner's" level. The 5-tile spriteSheet provides a more challenging game.

"Create" Essential Functions – Lines 89 to 136

Again nothing new here either. The "create" essential function displays the game's assets (unique to Phaser Gaming Framework).

- Lines 91 to 94 — are text styling.
- Lines 95 to 101 — binds the Phaser Gaming Framework to our "Pure JavaScript" game mechanics. What's odd is that the Phaser

Game Framework is telling the "Game Mechanics" the display information. Doing this "reverse" logic provides the ultimate flexibility in the **Collapsing Block** game mechanics. It is the game framework management of the display that has the restrictions, and so the "gaming framework" should set boundaries for the game mechanics.

- Lines 107 — consults the game state found in the game mechanics and "draws" the gameboard in line 111.
- Line 109 — creates a "listener" for the gamer's input.
- Lines 122 to 135 — manages the legal notice and copyrights display.

PlayGame.drawGameBoard – Lines 141 to 156

- Line 142 creates an array for "re-usable tiles".
- Lines 145 to 155 are standard double loop for populating a 2D grid. Phaser III has splendid internal support for automatically creating grids. Refer to:

  - https://phaser.io/examples/v3/view/game-objects/shapes/grid
  - https://rexrainbow.github.io/phaser3-rex-notes/docs/site/gridtable/
  - https://photonstorm.github.io/phaser3-docs/Phaser.GameObjects.Grid.html
  - https://phaser.io/examples/v3/view/game-objects/tilemap/static/grid-movement

PlayGame.tileSelect – Lines 158 to 190

- Refer to **https://makingbrowsergames.com/starterkits/collapsingblocks/v3.x.x/game.js**. This method prepares the playing field (aka game board) based on the game state stored inside the Game Mechanics class. It cycles through each row and column and assigns a random tile to a cell with its properties.
- Line 160: create and sets up this method.

- Line 161 to 162: creates internal working variables and validates selections.
- Line 163: Determines if it is possible to select a cell within the 2D grid.
- Line 163 to 190: Discovers the row of the selected tile. Discovers the column of the selected tile and then calculates its location through helper functions.

PlayGame.makeTilesFall – Lines 192 to 248

- Refer to https://makingbrowsergames.com/starterkits/collapsingblocks/v3.x.x/game.js.
- Lines 193 to 198 — prepared internal variables and consults the Game Mechanics game state to "arrange the Board after a Match".
- Lines 202 to 215 — is exclusive to the Phaser III framework tweens.
- Lines 217 to 241 — now that the tiles have fallen, it's time to replenish the gameboard from the top. These lines are exclusive to the Phaser III framework tweens.

PlayGame.makeTilesSlide – Lines 250 to 276

This method compacts and consolidates the column by sliding them to the left. It calls a "helper" method found in the Game Mechanics Component — compactBoardToLeft. I could elect to compact the play area to any side by simply providing parameters or creating separate methods.

PlayGame.endOfMove – Lines 277 to 304

We need one last check after tiles have fallen and were replenished to ensure that the game should continue. If all the groups remaining are less than two, the score is recorded, and in seven seconds the game restarts. Otherwise, if the gameboard is empty, we tell them about it.

5.3 Collapsing Blocks Game Mechanics Component

Now that we've separated all the unique Phaser Gaming Framework from the Collapsing Blocks genre rules and logic, let's explore our Game Mechanics Component.

The common characteristic of Game Mechanics are:

- storage of game state data.
- handles rules and logic — the "WHAT" to record and seek; **NOT HOW to display** the information (that's the job of the Gaming Framework).

Refer to **https://makingbrowsergames.com/starterkits/collapsingblocks/v3.x.x/game.js**.

- Lines 310 to 551 — hold all the "ES6 class" methods; all properties are stored inside its "constructor". If you're concerned about gamers hacking your game, you might consider testing for and setting the initial game parameters.

Inserted Hack Prevention

```
313    class cBlockGM{
314        // ---------------------------------------------------------
315        // constructor, simply turns obj information into class propertie
    s
316        constructor(obj){
317            if(obj == undefined) {
318                obj = {};        // gamer's hacking & prevention
319            }
320            // Set default values (hard-coded?) if missing
321            this.rows = (obj.rows != undefined) ? obj.rows : 10;
322            this.columns = (obj.columns != undefined) ? obj.columns : 20;
323            this.items = (obj.items != undefined) ? obj.items : 4;
324            // this parameter toggles for tiles exist off the bottom
325            this.fallingDown = (obj.fallingDown != undefined) ?
326                    obj.fallingDown : true;
327        }
```

- `alreadyVisited(row, column)` — tracks whether a cell is already in the "flood-fill" array and if so, returns "true".

- `arrangeBoardAfterMatch()` — prepares the game area after matching groups are tag as "empty" and records the changes to update the new game area.
- `createGameBoard()` — initially creates the game area data structure and records each cell's individual properties. Phaser III has several unique ways to create 2D grids. Refer to the notes on lines 361 to 364.
- `compactBoardToLeft()` — compacts the empty columns to the left. I could make this more dynamic by supplying a "direction" for compression or simply create and call individual methods for each direction. The first option is more flexible and does **NOT** assume a "square" (i.e., 4-sided) game board.
- `countConnectedItems(row, column)` — is called from the `playGame.tileSelect` method. This helper supplies "how many" similar tiles are in the group.
- `countLeftEmptyColumns(column)` — returns how many empty columns to shift.
- `emptySpacesBelow(row, column)` — returns how many empty spaces are below a cell.
- `floodFill(row, column)` — there are 5 different algorithms for managing "flood-fill" operations. This uses the simplest. See the notes at line 438.
- `getColumns()` — superfluous method when consulting the constructor would be minimally sufficient.
- `getCustomDataAt(row, column)` — returns the specific property characteristics of a cell.
- `getRows()` — another superfluous method when consulting the constructor would be minimally sufficient.
- `getValueAt(row, column)` — another superfluous method when consulting the `getCustomDataAt` would be minimally sufficient.
- `isEmpty(row, column)` — returns the cell state whether it is occupied or empty.

- `listConnectedItems(row, column)` — returns an array of similar cell values surrounding the selected cell.
- `removeConnectedItems(row, column)` — simply toggles a specific cell to the "empty" state.
- `replenishBoard()` — repopulates empty cells with newly generated information, and changes cell state to "occupied".
- `setCustomData(row, column, customData)` — writes cell characteristics. Called from initial gameboard creation and replenish.
- `swapItems(row, column, row2, column2)` — called from `arrangeBoardAfterMatch` and `compactBoardToLeft` to shift data properties.
- `validPick(row, column)` — filters erroneous cell selections.

7 Game Shell - The CMS!

Now that our "play phase" works. Let's surround our game with a "game shell" — all those auxiliary business-driver functions we discussed earlier. Remember, once we create a "game shell" for a game, nothing changes in the "shell"; it's D.R.Y. until you change your business objectives *or (hint, hint) license (or lease) your game using "white-label" deployments!*

7.1 Generic Main.js

Let's review each JavaScript file in the skeleton header. The `main.js` file *"IS"* the game's mechanics component, it's the foundation, game logic, mechanics, rules, and configuration information. It holds all the background stories, any "factory" generators, the game settings used during the "play phase". What you entitle this file is not critical, but always name it the same across all your projects. Why? Because we have a "D.R.Y." thing going on and we want to "stay dry" —to keep our consistency across all our development projects and conserve our development time. There's another reason:

NAMESPACE SECURITY! As players launch and play our collection of games, one game will "over-write" another in the client-side cache.

I take a "less formal" approach than before inside mobile versions. As explained earlier for mobile single web page applications (SWPA), I insert the entire raw `main.js` script *as an inline script tag.* Yes, there are problems with this technique, and you should become aware of *Why should I Avoid Inline scripting?*

Review a *generic version* of this file with language transformations or a **classful version here**.

Each chapter tutorial might have unique changes; you can download a sample of those specific genre changes from this chapter. Review the demonstration games from each chapter and open your browser console to watch how the Phaser Game Framework interacts.

7.2 Generic Boot.js

Our boot state was launched from our "`index.html`" page. This game phase has the responsibility of configuring and setting up the "`html5 canvas`" and game physics. As the name suggests, its purpose prepares the web browser and sets the game dimensions — loading various game assets and storing them in the local Phaser cache, and having them readily available when needed throughout the game. Once the canvas is prepared and sized to fit the display dimensions, it will typically hands-off control toward the next phase called the "`load`" phase. Since this file is sometimes so small, I'll "in-line" the script inside the "`index.html`" page to avoid an additional download. This is an especially important concept for mobile games. Here's an article that discusses the *advantages and disadvantages* of "in-line scripts". Once again, it's your choice.

"If we create new graphics files, but call them by the same names we have in our game shell. We simply replace the game art with new art (with the same file names) and VOILA! NEW GAME ... same mechanics, same source code, yet with different "look &

feel" — this is the secret sauce for cranking out a game per week." This means you have to stay within the existing sizes of every graphical asset. For example, a button is fixed in its dimensions and position within the code. You shouldn't change that. But you can change the design of your button theme, as you should do with every visual asset in your game. You could make the new artwork smaller since that won't change the predefined borders allocated for that button. However, if you make it bigger, it will be automatically cropped. You'll need to re-dimension that visual space — generating more work to do. "Measure twice, cut once" from the carpenter's motto applies to games too — "measure your layout with due consideration, and publish it once."

Some game developers take a "more formal" approach and split each internal game phase into distinct classifications or module files (for example `missiles.js`, `avatar.js`, `enemyships.js`, `gameHandler.js`, ad nauseam). They do this during development to easily find and squash those nasty software bugs. Then, when they're ready to release their game, they use various *tools to obfuscate, minify, and merge* all those separate modules back into a single "monolithic" game file again — just as we have done here already!

In our mobile SWPA & PWA demonstration examples found on the book's website, we collapsed everything into a single file called `game.js` as a "single web page application" (SWPA) mobile version. In our *CodeIgniter Content Management system (CMS)* demonstration (PWA), I took a more formal approach leading to the game page where Phaser canvas displays.

Boot.js internal functions

- `init` function — prepares critical variables for game usage
- `preload` function — downloads all the game assets.
- `create` function — manages the game size (min and max), alignment, **local browser storage**, and input.

- `enableScaling` function — fits the game into the current window dimensions. You can also re-size your game to fit the browser window from the new `config` object parameters. Here's *another clever way* to re-size your game.

- `enterIncorrectOrientation` function — notify gamer to rotate their device.

- `leaveIncorrectOrientation` function — adjust the game to the device's orientation.

Boot.js auxiliary and supporting functions

- `firstRun` — local and session storage management.

- `initScoreSystem` — manages scoreboard reset, retrieves "sounds (sfx)" settings from local storage, initializes local keyboard settings, and retrieves gamer's language.

- `resetLeaderboard` — sets a pseudo leader board from localized data.

- `getKeyName` — Keyboard management and default settings.

- `loadUserKeys` — configurable user keyboard loaded from local storage.

- `saveUserKeys` — saves new keyboard configuration for non-QWERTY layouts in local storage.

- `getDefaultUserKeys` — retrieves default `Phaser.Keyboard` settings.

Review a *generic version of this file* here or a **classful version here**.

7.3 Generic Preload.js

This Game Phase manages our file downloads; you should optimize this process with the fewest downloads immediately required by your game. I sometimes "inline" the normal "`boot.js`" into the "`index.html`" and combined everything else into a "`game.js`"; doing so, defers several potential downloaded files with this single combined file. For example, I "inlined" the normal "`boot.js`" into the "`index.html`" and merged everything else into the "`play.js`". Many developers use **Webpack** or **Parcel** to the same effect. The formal-style and separate "`preload.js`" now becomes a simple JavaScript object inside a single web page application (SWPA) illustrated in the Introduction Section.

Example: **Preload.js internalized** as a JavaScript Object

```
1       // =========================================
2       // --------------------------------------
3       // Supporting Game Function
4       // --------------------------------------
5       //**TODO**:
6       // - Change the generic GAMEAPP to your project name
7       // - refactor and adjust for your game deployment
8       // - remove console debug information on public deployment
9       // =========================================
10      // act as a Preload.js, preloads graphics and enable scaling
11      function onPreload() {
12
13          game.load.spritesheet("tiles","assets/sqLites.png",36,35);
14          // Phaser v3: this.load.spritesheet( ..... )
15
16          game.scale.scaleMode = Phaser.scaleManager.SHOW_ALL;
17          // Phaser v3: scales within the configuration object.
18          // Phaser v2.x.x deprecated: game.scale.setscreensize(true);
19          // replace with:
20          game.scale.refresh();
21
22          //debug
23          console.log("Game Assets loaded and re-scaled");
24      }
```

Preload.js essential functions

- `preload function` — manages game assets downloads
- `create function` — prepares a download bar and progress

Review a *generic version of this file* here or a **classful version here**.

7.4 Generic Splash.js or Language.js

Finally, we arrive at our splash phase — hopefully within 20 seconds; if our game takes longer than 20 seconds to activate, it stands rejection from most "app stores". Here is an excellent place to inform our gamers about our sponsorships, provide advertisements

(? **HONESTLY!** If you don't like them, your clients won't either! See the statistics on "Ad Blockers" in Phaser Game Design Workbook page 232, "In-Game Purchases"), offer language selections and present your own branding and logos. While your gamer pauses to select their language, it allows more time to download more game assets *or (better yet!) launch your game's web socket connection.* This phase further allows another place to set theme mood-music, provide a background narrative, and such. Again, a word of caution here, all "app store" require your game to be "live and active" within 20 seconds. Read this *"Special Report - DEC 2018"* on EU Internet Access Speeds.

What I do is present a "language menu" to our gamers and let them select — *dynamically on-demand!!* — their native language for continued game-play and interaction. I won't download every language lexicon known to mankind; and, of course, *we'll steer clear of "Enochian"* … we'll have none of that here; they can go "somewhere else and play".

The natural choice for language selection is a button mechanism designed around the gamer's national flag — *"iconic symbols" ARE the international language.* (This is the reason many game distributors will reject games with internal text; they want internationally "understood" symbols.) When our gamer glides over any nation's flag, a "`tool-tip text`" changes into that nation's predominant language. Mesmerized by the sudden display of various languages and spellings, our gamer — **doing what they do best (i.e.: to play)** — might spend, perhaps, a whole 3-seconds goofing around, thus providing us more time for downloading game resources *through perhaps a newly activated web socket.* Naturally, there must be a different method to handle mobile "touch/roll-over" input. Clever as our gamers are, they will "`select-click`" the flag button representing their native language as a visual clue. On that "`click-event`", the internal game functions will send a request to download that specific "`JSON`" language file that will dynamically populate (e.g.: substitute) all text variables inside our game. Read some interesting facts about the Internet and **who your "real" target audience is becoming!**

Sample Main Menu

For our Mobile SWPA/PWA, we'll use another "`<div>`" tag inside the "`index.html`" file. Review the mobile "`index.html`" source code, and you find that the "splash phase" is merely a "`<div>`" tag using Bootstrap CSS!

Modifications for the "`Splash.js`" or "`Language.js`" should be minimal as long as you have a standard information and *menuing system* across all your games. Loading the standard game phase menus, images, and buttons are already listed. There should not be anything in this file you would need to modify nor change ... unless we have a new sponsorship (e.g., white-label) or adding new targeted languages.

You will discover tools such as *PoEdit* or *locize* beneficial in creating JSON files to substitute all text variables within your game. Both of these translation services allow you to edit your game's text into

JSON format for "i18next". The advantage of using such tools is that it's easier to contract vendors for work on your text translations.

Fortunately, there is a **Phaser III plugin** we have adopted that works with "i18next" — **an internationalization i18n-framework written in and for JavaScript.** This plugin allows us to have seamless translations in any of our games. It integrates "i18next" for translation management, which is widely adopted by the JS community at large in other projects as well.

Its key features are:

- Support for translations namespaces,
- Simple key/value JSON,
- Seamless switching of languages,
- No extra function calls for translating strings, directly built into Phaser's Text object.

For our Mobile SWPA game, we use the index.html file. Review the source code, and you find that the "splash phase" is merely a "div" tag using Bootstrap CSS.

You can try a live demonstration from **https://makingbrowsergames.com/p3gp-book/_p3-arrav15/index.html**

Some game distributors will reject games with any displayed text. They want simple symbols with a "globally understood meaning".

Review a *generic version of this file* here or a **classful version here**.

7.5 Generic Menu.js

Our next screen is the game's "main menu". Usually, we divide our game into various levels of difficulty (depending on your game's genre and how you might plan to design it). In the *Phaser Game Design Workbook*, I go into greater depth on work-flow, how to load scripts (sync, async or deferred), and the use of internationalization (language selections).

Modification to this file should be minimal also so long as you have a standard menu system across all games. Loading the standard game phase menus, images, and buttons are already listed. There should not be anything in this file you need to modify nor change. During my game development, I've come up with new business models and ideas. In earlier versions, I had a short story that would lead directly to the game-play. My current versions (since 2015) combine those "short story narratives" inside the "`main menu`".

- **Older version 1992 to 2008** online example.
- **From 2008 to Present** (Content Management system (CMs), game-shell, and PWA game-styles allow for greater flexibility in supporting information and lightens the load of the Phaser `canvas` for any version.)

On the main menu, you should offer your gamers several options before starting their game's play in earnest. The following scripts are not included and would be better handled as, perhaps, separate HTML web pages in a content management system.

Menu.js internal functions

- `preload` function — not used; everything was downloaded in the boot.js
- `create` function — links downloaded assets for use during the game.
- `beginGame` function — manages theme music
- `gameCredits` function — manages theme music and game author information
- `moreGame` function — manages theme music, and provides access to more games from the author.

You can try a demonstration from
https://makingbrowsergames.com/p3gp-book/standalone/js/state/menu.js

On the main menu, you should offer your gamers several options before starting their game-play in earnest. The following scripts are not included and would be better handled as separate HTML web pages in a content management system. Visit **http://www.adventurers-of-renown.com/quests/arra.php** as an example of a **Content Management System (CodeIgniter CMS).**

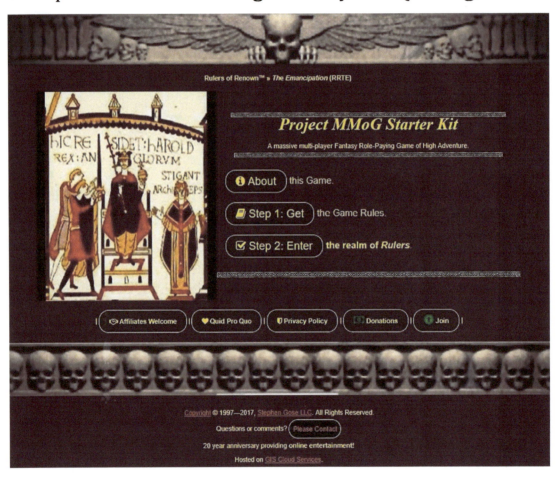

Simple CMS or PWA Game Shell

Typical pages within a Content Management System (CMS) are not directly related to the game mechanics nor gameplay. These pages enhance and support several business aspects and develop customer loyalty. For example, visit http://www.adventurers-of-renown.com/quests/arra.php as an example of a Content Management system (CMS):

Sample Main Menu

- `About.js` — a page biography to enhance your portfolio and resume. In our mobile demonstration, the `about page` is used to enhance SEO and page content since it is simply just another `<div>` tag.

- `Credits.js` — a page giving attributions.

- `Donations.js` — a page requesting financial support linking to your PayPal.me, Patreon, IndieGoGo, Kickstarter, and *other crowd-funding pages*.

- `Instructions.js` or `help.js` — a page offering helpful hints, walk-throughs, achievement, awards, entitlements, or game rules. If the game instructions are minimal in content, it could be combined with another page. Instructions should never appear in simple "casual games".

- `Language.js` — a page offering gamers text in their native language.

- `MoreGame.js` — a redirection page to your whole collection of games; used to build a loyal fan base. This is just smart business acumen; this technique is found in the most successful games.
- `Options.js` — a configuration page used to set or re-map keyboard input, and the like.
- `Scores.js` — pulls from a master database of recorded scores.
- `Share.js` — a page to enhance the viral distribution of your game or announcements within the game. ***See twitter enhancement.***
- `SubmitScores.js` — collects and transmits the current game session for permanent storage.
  - `wins.js` — records information into the gamer's registered account.
  - `Lose.js` — records information into the gamer's registered account.
- `WebMasters.js` — a page offering license and distribution information.

Review a ***generic version of this file*** here or a **classful version here**.

Sample CMS page — Credits.js

The acknowledgment and credits page plays an important role in any game and its license. It is the contact information for you, your contributors, sponsors, and a source of advertisement.

We have a choice in its deployment. We could dynamically generate the page content on each visit OR build a static image. I chose the latter since it is a sponsored advertisement for Jester Costumes displayed throughout the game. The disadvantage of displaying this scene as an image is that the text is static and in English only.

- `create function` — links downloaded assets to display
- `update function` — not used.
- `quitGame function` — returns to the main menu

Credit Scene as Static Image with Sponsor information

NOTE: You can download this file from
https://makingbrowsergames.com/starterkits/quiz/p3game2/index.html

Review this file; it is thoroughly annotated and documented to reduce the price of this pamphlet.

Deeper Dive: Using JAMStack as an SSG …

Static websites aren't new! They were what everyone once built before dynamic **CMS**s (e.g., WordPress, Drupal, Joomla, etc.) took over at the start of the millennium.

Content management can be challenging for end-users who don't have a technical background. The good news is there's an impressive number of **headless CMSs** out there ready to complete your **"Static Site Generation" (SSG).** The differences between "headless" and "traditional" CMSs are that you'll use the former only for "content management" tasks, not templating and front-end content generation such as the Phaser Gaming Framework.

JAMstack stands for ***JavaScript, API, Markup (JAM).*** Quoted from 'Introducing JAMstack: The Modern Web Architecture':
"JAMstack projects don't rely on server-side code, they can be distributed instead of relying on a server. Served directly from a CDN, JAMstack apps unlock speed, performance, and better user experience. ... Unlike traditional websites or CMS sites (e.g WordPress, Drupal, etc.) that relies so much on servers, plugins, and databases, JAMstack can load some JavaScript that receives data from an API, serving files from a CDN and markup generated using a static site generator during deploy time."

When we talk about "The Stack," we no longer talk about operating systems, specific web servers, backend programming languages, or databases.

The *JAMStack* is not about specific technologies. It's a new way of building websites and apps that delivers better performance, higher security, lower cost of scaling, and a better developer experience.

Pre-rendered sites can be enhanced with JavaScript and the growing capabilities of browsers and services available via APIs.

Deeper Dive: Static Site Generators (SSG)

Knowing what ***Static Site Generators (SSG)*** are and why you should use them is one thing; knowing which one to adopt is an entirely different story. There are over 400+ available. You might visit *staticgen.com* and be overwhelmed with choices. Or investigate:

- *Grav* — a modern open-source flat-file CMS and "Markdown" editor. Website *skeletons available here*. You might even consider using *Grav tied to Gatsby*.
- *PICO* — "Pico is a stupidly simple, blazing fast, flat file CMS. That's definitely a mouthful, what does it even mean? In the most basic sense, it means that there is no administration back-end or database to deal with. ***You simply create markdown files*** in the

content folder and those files become your pages. There's much more to Pico than that though."

- **Error! Hyperlink reference not valid.** — "Gatsby brings static pages to front-end stacks, leveraging client-side JavaScript, reusable APIs, and pre-built "Markup". It's an easy-to-use solution that creates a SPA (Single Page Application) … *Gatsby.js is a static PWA (Progressive Web App) generator."* *See example here*

Exercise: Adopting *the best SSG* for your game project.

7.6 Inside each Game Phase

Phaser v3 permits multiple "scenes" inside a single "Game Phase". This is an incredibly powerful feature. In the Game Play Phase below, I am using 5 different "scenes": the gameboard, the player's input menu, the game feedback at the bottom, and the left-hand HUD. Each of these "scenes" is independent and managed separately in Phaser v3. **It reminds me of MovieClips in Flash game development.**

Rogue Prince - *5 Scenes displayed in the "Play Phase"!*

Each of these scenes we discussed above has **"its own internal essential functions" to manage its "life-cycle".** These internal functions *are common to all Phaser versions.* These functions give a way to organize our code into separate objects (or ES6 "Fat Arrow Functions") and ensure that only the minimal game assets (for this current game phase) are supplied at just the proper time. A "Phaser v3 Scene" helps us isolate distinct sections from each other inside a Game Phase. In my mind, **Phaser 3 Scenes are similar to Adobe Flash "MovieClips"** running on the timeline ("Game Phase"). For example, booting the game; loading assets; main menu; playing levels one, winning, losing, are all game phases that **might be** a "Phaser single scene". **This is an important concept in the new Phaser v3 since game scenes in Phaser v3 are far more autonomous than v2.x.x.** And unlike Phaser v2.x.x, you can have *multiple scenes active at the same time* in Phaser 3. The goal we achieve, by using this "finite state machine" structure as game phases, makes our game development simpler and less painful to support.

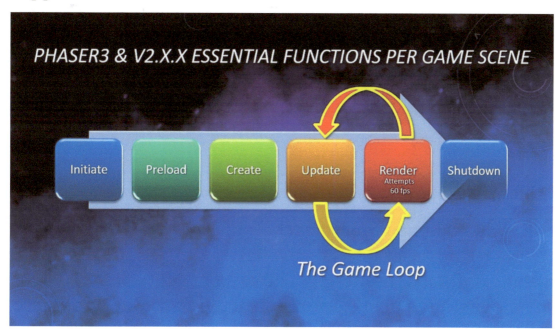

Phaser Essential "Life-cycle" Functions

- The **"Initiate"** (or Boot) sets-up current variables, canvas dimensions, browser orientation, and data **for this specific game phase.**
- The **"Preload"** method manages all the game assets, downloading, and storing them in the Phaser Cache.
- The **"Create"** method makes the downloaded game assets available to the display list.
- The **"Update"** method attempts to collect the "whereabouts" of all the game assets on the stage (aka "camera view") at approximately 60 frames per second (fps). In Phaser v3, you now have the option to manage the "frame-per-second" (fps) using the "Tween Manager". For example, setting the frame rate updates to 15 fps would look like this:

Sample from *Phaser III Snake.js*

```
1    // From http://labs.phaser.io/index.html?dir=games/snake/&q=
2    var config = {
```

```
3          type: Phaser.AUTO,
4          width: SCREEN_SIZE * SPRITE_SIZE,
5          height: SCREEN_SIZE * SPRITE_SIZE,
6          fps: {
7              target: FRAMES_PER_SECOND, // a constant set elsewhere!
8          },
9          physics: {
10             default: "arcade",
11             arcade: {
12                 fps: FRAMES_PER_SECOND
13             }
14         },
15         scene: [ SnakeGameScene ],
16     };
```

Review the *discussions on setting frame rates*.

- The **"Render"** method publishes the game asset's new positions on the stage. In Phaser v3, you now have a choice of either "dynamic" or "static" rendering. The responsibility of the "Game Loop", as illustrated below, is to control the flow of several game elements during gameplay. The "Game Loop" is a standard "universal process" of **"input, process, and output" (IPO).** It re-cycles until the game migrates to the "Game Over" phase — "game won" or "game lost". The Phaser v3 "game loop" has many moving parts inside, and the render phase attempts to maintain a rate of 60 frames per second (fps).

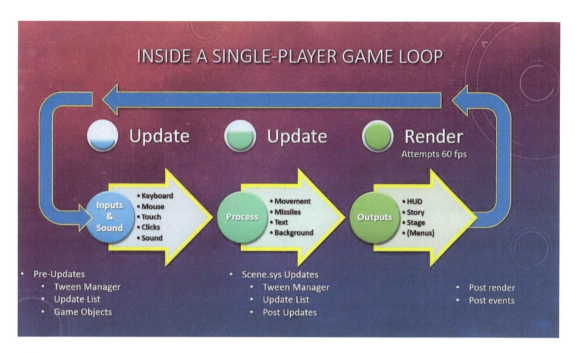

Phaser v3 Game Loop

8 Plug-in Enhancements

It's nice that so many people write content for Phaser.js Gaming Framework. You can search GitHub and find thousands of add-on, plugins, and enhancements for either version. I'd like to recommend one I recently found from "rantt_". It is a *"Twitter button"*; learn how he's integrated it into his projects.

Phaser v3 Twitter Plugin

```
1      //Phaser Twitter
2      var config = {
3          type: Phaser.AUTO,
4          parent: 'phaser-example',
5          width: 800,
6          height: 500,
7          scene: {
8              preload: preload,
9              create: create
10         }
11     };
12
13     var game = new Phaser.Game(config);
```

```
14
15    function preload () {
16        this.load.image('tweet', 'assets/twitter.png');
17    }
18
19    function create () {
20        var btnTweet = this.add.image(400, 250, 'tweet').setInteractive();
21        btnTweet.on('pointerup', openExternalLink, this);
22    }
23
24    function openExternalLink () {
25        var tweetTxt = 'I am testing my new MMoG Game on Twitter';
26        var url = 'https://twitter.com/intent/tweet?
27                    text=' + encodeURIComponent(tweetTxt);
28        var s = window.open(url, '_blank');
29
30        if (s && s.focus) {
31            s.focus();
32        } else if (!s) {
33            window.location.href = url;
34        }
35    }
```

See other *excellent Phaser Plugins* for either version from this brilliant engineer.

9 Conclusion

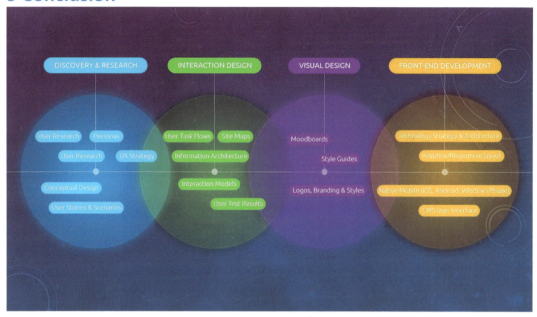

Software Project Management

We are at the end of game development and should deploy our game into the wild. Topics such as launch times, download times, *time to first byte* (TTFB), domain naming servers (DNS) "lookups", all these now come into our business project's scope.

When you launch your *"Golden Release"*, it is critical that we "collapse" all our module files into as few as possible, obfuscate them and minify them using **Webpack** or **Parcel** to protect our "intellectual property". I recommend several of these tools found in this workbook. "How to use such tools?", you say? Take a side-trip to this fantastic article.[1]

10 Bonus Development Content

Earn your game developer certifications! Access your *FREE Online course* included with this book. Use the coupon link below and start your course today.

- **"Phaser Game Design Workshop"** — **Making Phaser v2.x.x Break-Out** — included with your book purchase, valued at $19.99, yours **FREE!**

https://leanpub.com/c/phasergamedesignworkshop/c/3IWDBydPFVj1

- **"Phaser III Game Design Workshop"** — **Making Phaser v3.15+ Break-Out** — included with your book purchase, valued at $19.99, yours **FREE!**

https://leanpub.com/c/p3gdc/c/Tx4iHQ6m64c5

- *Critical Rendering Path* — Free course *sponsored by Udacity (here)*.
- GG Interactive — *FREE Game Design course*.

What's next?

10.1 Game Distribution & Marketing

Short Excerpt from the *Phaser Game Design Workbook*.

"How to publish a game on the web??"

Quoted from the Unity forum
Hello, I have a little problem with the publishing thing. I've created a little "game", which has only one scene and exported it as a web game. OK, now I have an HTML and Unity 3d files. But, the problem is, **I don't know anything about creating websites, or uploading files to servers.** I know that there are several questions about this, but I just can't understand what to do. I would really appreciate it if someone could explain to me **how to publish my "game" on the web step by step.** By the way, I've created a **WIX site,** but I'm not sure if I can put a Unity 3d game in there. *Read answers here*

I forbid my students from using **WIX** when attempting to "showcase" their Web Developer or Gaming Programming Skills in their portfolios.

Introduction: 8-Step Deployment Method.

1. Research game publishers. Learn who they are, what games they favor, and who their target audience is. Be careful when analyzing Return On Investments (ROI). *This article* gives a proper perspective.

2. Contact those publishers, discover their submission policies and requirements for Software Development Kit (SDK) usage. Read carefully about surrendering your rights. Learn what game genre peek their interests. However, be careful not to lock yourself in and become entirely dependent on a single company's SDK for your entire marketing strategy. I learned my lesson from the MochiMedia collapse. While there's **no doubt you should integrate** a tracking SDK to register conversions, I recommend that you keep tracking and usage analytics technically distinct from your advertising collection management, to remain flexible and be able to switch partners if you are not satisfied with the results.

3. Create your game .... *(duh!) You can't sell "blue-sky" ideas.*

4. Create *a domain name and game website.* (**NOTE:** Some ISPs *include a 1-year FREE domain name* with their web hosting packages.) Demonstrate your game prototype(s) to their buyers in a protected section of your website — as an example *click here.*

5. Refine your game mechanics. Get *strangers (non-developers with their "gut reactions")* and other *indie developers* to play it. An excellent place to find fellow developers is in the new *Phaser Forum*. They'll find problems you may have overlooked. Naturally, you'll want to fix those errors they find.

6. Deploy the latest obfuscated/compacted game version on your public website.

7. Wait ... wait ... read their feedback and if necessary return to step #1. Otherwise, continue to step #8.
8. Negotiate a contract *wisely.* Your new publisher might require the use of their Software Development Kit (SDK).
9. Start your next game project(s). ... return to Step #1

Shareably (SBLY) **looking to rent your Phaser games**

SBLY is looking for new game titles to add to their platform through rental sponsorships ($50 - $100 per month) and possibly non-exclusive or exclusive licensing deals.

SBLY is fairly new to the web game space, but by no means new to publishing. They started in 2015 and have now amassed over 50 million monthly readers across their publishing networks. Finding early success in this space they now believe that bringing on new titles from other developers is a worthwhile investment. Your game will be on their publishing site https://shareably.net although this will transition to a new domain in the coming months.

SBLY's product lead engineer, John Lee, explains: "We like the rental sponsorships because we can quickly see if your game will succeed with low commitment early on and of course, developers are free to do this with many other publishers!

As for games, I'm particularly looking for familiar games (Minesweeper, FreeCell, spider solitaire, matching games, etc) right now, but in the future, we'll be open to all categories so please don't hesitate to reach out so we can get the conversations rolling."

If you're interested, you can reach John at john@sbly.com, or on the Phaser Discord (@jawnwee)

10.2 Book Review Protocol

Did you "like" or "learn" anything from this Book?

If you liked this book, it would mean the world to me if you took just a moment to leave an **honest positive review** on your "book distributor's review page".

Remember, you can earn commissions by recommending this book through your affiliate links!

If **your opinion is less than 3 stars out of 5,** please allow me to make amends before you "publically crucify me" and tell me what you believe is missing *in a personal one-on-one email.* I've learned that "poor reviews" from "angry readers" were **never revisited and updated by them** after I've made those corrections in the following book's editions. Those belligerent comments only make the reviewer appear vindictive when the newest edition has those corrections.

E-Mail me at (https://leanpub.com/makingjump2capturebrowsergames/email_author/new) with the "Subject: Book concerns – (the book title)". Please provide, in your email message body:

- the page number, and
- supporting evidence from *primary technical references* that support your opinion(s). (Sorry, I don't consider "rumors", "crowd following", "comments from forums" and *any unsubstantiated opinions — even if you do hold a Ph.D. or have "a gazillion years" of experience)*
- allow me *sufficient time to respond with an updated book edition — which I will email directly to you in a DRM .pdf format.*
- THEN, provide your rating (or update your rating if you didn't follow my request?!) to 3+.

10.3 Tell the world about *your* game!

Excellent! You completed this workbook and constructed your game. Do you want to brag about your additional features or unique modifications? Do you have additional features or game "tweaks" you want to show to the world? Then, let me use your creation in up-coming articles **and book edition updates! Earn the popularity you deserve!**

Use this contact email:

- E-Mail me at (*https://leanpub.com/makingjump2capturebrowsergames/email_author/new*) with the "Subject: Game Show Case - (your game's title)". Please provide, in your email:
- the book you read to develop your bespoke game edition. **(hint: use your affiliate link and earn commissions!)**
- a list of your game's unique and/or innovations.
- a website URL to play your demo or licensed versions.

Appendix

Excellent! You completed this workbook and constructed your game. Still hungry for more? Take some time and review the following resources.

More Resources

JavaScript Garden

JavaScript Garden is a **growing collection of documentation about the most quirky parts of the JavaScript programming language. It advises how to avoid common mistakes and subtle bugs, as well as performance issues and bad practices, that non-**

expert JavaScript programmers may encounter on their endeavors into the depths of the language.

JavaScript Garden does not aim to teach you JavaScript. Former knowledge of the language is strongly recommended to understand the topics covered in this guide. To learn the basics of the language, please head over to the excellent guide on the Mozilla Developer Network.

Additional Content Appendices

Available Bonus Content has 67-pages of **external downloads.**

- *Appendix: Building HTML5 Web Page (3-pages)*
- *Appendix: Distribution Channels (2-pages)*
- *Appendix: Game Design Considerations (1-page)*
- *Appendix: Game Design Overview (3-pages)*
- *Appendix: Game Resources and References (17-pages)*
- *Appendix: JS Coding Styles (7-pages)*
- *Appendix: Networking (9-pages)*
- *Appendix: Phaser 3 Resources (2-pages)*
- *Appendix: Project Management Analysis (13-pages)*
- *Appendix: Security (5-pages)*
- *Appendix: US Business Start-ups (4-pages)*
- **FREE** Phaser III *Game Developer Course*
- *Facebook Game AI & WebXR Developers*
- *Facebook Game Developers*

Other resources:
- *Phaser FAQ* **OR** *Phaser Discord*
- *Phaser Plugins (.com)* 121+ Phaser Plugins (as of 20191001) for either v2.x.x or III.
- 9-slice: https://github.com/jdotrjs/phaser3-nineslice

- *Pathbuilder* — A tool to build paths for Pathfollowers and path tweens. Draw and edit Lines, Bezier Curves, Splines, and Ellipses during runtime and export them to Phaser.
- *Weapons Plugin* — A Phaser v3 compatible port of the Weapon Plugin shipped with Phaser v2.x.x. The author considers this plugin is stable and mostly feature complete. Most bugs should be fixed, but if any do occur please help us by reporting them.
- **Phaser 3 Ninepatch Plugin** — Phaser3 Nine Patch plugin adds 9-slice scaling support to Phaser 3 by Koreezgames
- **Generic Platformer and Phaser Bootstrap Project** — Generic platformer and Phaser 3 bootstrap project

Selling your Game Assets

This is similar to *selling a car in parts* from a "hack-shop". See how *AppGameKit* manages their *"piecemeal"* sales.

- Sell your knowledge, discoveries, concepts, and designs as *tutorials, ebooks, guides, and courses (examples here)*.
- Sell your *3D Models here* or from my favorite 3D publisher *DAZ 3D* download their *FREE DAZ 3D Studio Manager*.
- *As a Commercial Game Starter Kits* (examples)
- *Creative Market* — is the world's marketplace for design. Bring your creative projects to life with ready-to-use design assets from independent creators around the world. **Sell your game assets.**
- *Envato Elements* — Sell your graphics, audio, images, plugins, themes, and videos.
- *Game Developer's Market* — GameDev Market (GDM) is a community-driven marketplace based in the UK that connects indie game developers with talented asset creators. There are asset stores specific to certain game engines, huge generic stock websites with an overwhelming catalog of assets of varying quality, and smaller indie stores with small selections of very niche assets.

- *HumbleBundle for Developers* — Humble games wants to make it easier for indie developers to succeed. Publishing is their way to give back to the indie community by helping great ideas to become successful games. They want to share their Humble Bundle's experience and international marketing scale to help every developer make more games and reach more customers. You can create your own webpage to showcase and sell your game. ***Hosting is free, and you keep 95% of the proceeds after payment processing and taxes.*** You can edit your page whenever you want, and you also have access to our customer support team. Get many of the features and benefits of their "Humble Gamepage" in a handy widget that ***you can add directly to your site to sell your game.*** Edit and customize it at any time, and ***keep 95% of proceeds*** after payment processing and taxes.

Appendix: Making WebXR games!

Refer to the following pioneers who are building 3D Phaser games.

- *Headless Game Design*
- *WebXR Device API Explained*
- *Making DOOM 3D in Phaser*
- *Enabled 3D for Web, Mobile, and PC*
- *Phaser III 3D Camera Plugin*
- *Phaser v3.5 Extern Code for Three.js*
- *34 3d examples in Phaser III*
- *Build fake 3D HTML5 games with Phaser, Arcade physics, three.js, and Phaser 3D library* advice from Emanuele Feronato
- *Super-Powers* — **2D and 3D game making for indies; Free and open-source.** Superpowers are powered by three.js, Socket.IO, TypeScript, Electron, Node.js, and many other lovely open-source projects.

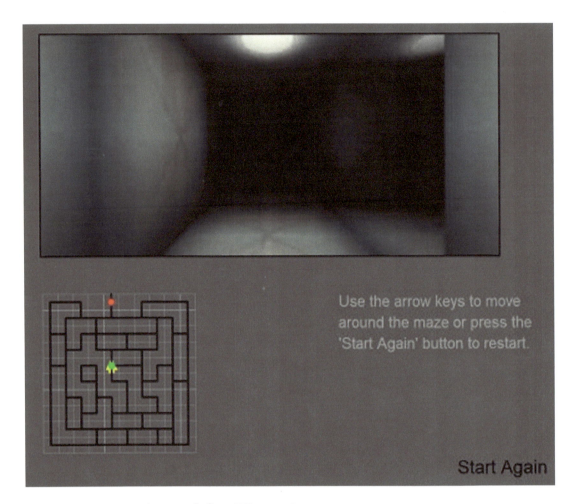

First-person view of the 3D environment

Appendix: Online Game Development

- *Modd.io* — Make a game in **3 days,** not in 3 months. Modd.io is running on a Multi-Player game engine with Box2d physics built-in. Many features have been put in place over the years such as client-side prediction and bandwidth optimization.

Appendix: Phaser III Plugins

I highly recommend *phaser3-rex-notes on GitHub* and *Awesome-phaser* as your first couple of stops for any Phaser III plugins. **Also,**

there is superior documentation located at
https://rexrainbow.github.io/phaser3-rex-notes/docs/site/
Current, as of the last visit, there are the following Phaser III available plugins: 20181211

- actions (Hexagon and Quad grid)
- audio (fade and midiplayer)
- behaviors (boid, bullet, 8-directions, fade, flash, interception, moveto, pathfollower, rotateto, scale, ship,textpage, texttyping)
- board (board, chess, grid, hexagonmap, match, miniboard, monopoly, moveto, pathfinder, shape utils)
- data (bank, csvtoarray, csvtohashtable, pool, restorabledata)
- gameobjects (bbocdtext, canvas, containerlite, gridtable, shape, tagtext)
- geom (hexagon, quad, rhombus, utils)
- input (button, cursoratbound, drag, dragscale, dragspeed, mousewheeltoupdonw, scroller, slider, touchsursor, touchstate, virtualjoystick)
- loader (awaitloader, webfontloader)
- logic (achievements, conditionstable, fsm, runcommands, waitevents)
- math/gashapon (Gashapon.js)
- shaders (pixelation, swirl)
- string (lzstring, xor)
- time (clock, lifetime)
- utils (… 25 total! in this directory)

Appendix: "How to Start a WebSocket"

Excerpt from Chapter 6
"Phaser Making Massive Multi-Player Online Games"

With the solid foundation from Parts I & II, your research, and answers to the various exercises, we are — at last! — ready to begin our source coding sessions. We will start on the client-side and migrate across the MMoG Architecture we discussed in Part II. Our goal, by the end of this chapter, is to have:

- a functional WebSocket conduit (aka "telecommunications channel") starting from client-side proxy to server API with data formatted as either an RPC or MOM. It becomes our MMoG prototype to expand into more specific game messages in later chapters.
- a guiding regimen showing us where to place our source code across our MMoG systems.

To use WebSockets, you need a browser, a web server, and a socket app server that all support *the same WebSocket protocol.* (You learned that in Part I, and *all the reasons* to avoid using Socket.IO and its incompatibilities). Your best friend will become the *"Can I Use" website*; it provides current information about the WebSocket technology, browsers to avoid, known issues, and resources. You were given two test sites in Part II; it's time to create your own testing server — this is not the same as a Web Server. You will need a traditional web server (such as Apache or IIS) on your local development workstation to serve your game's *dynamic content.* (You'll recall from Part I that Node.js and Express only deliver static content? Right?) You have a "Project Game Starter Kit" in your Bonus Content you need to copy this into your workstations web server root directory and make sure it's running in the background of your development workstation. You'll need to make sure not to close the command prompt window!

Exercise: Download the "Project-GameStarterKit":

https://makingbrowsergames.com/mmog/bonusContent/WebSockets.zip or any client SDK from *https://kaazing.com/download/*

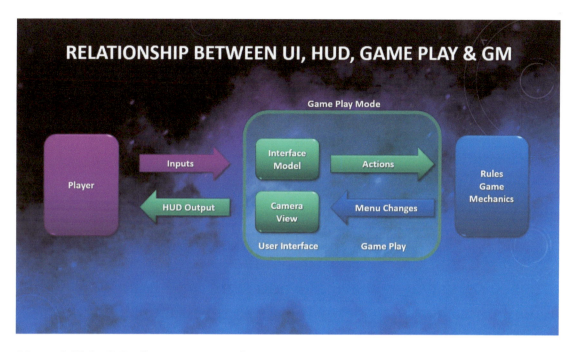

New MMoG Information Flow

The Client-side has several important responsibilities while processing the game logic so that it works well with the remote server (or local proxy server) and provides a quality game-play experience:

- **Rendering** — the Client-side is responsible for rendering the game on the player's display, and may be responsible for non-important physics simulations, such as cloth simulations or particle effect — such special effects (sfx) should **NOT** come from a remote server, **RIGHT?** If a client-side animation doesn't have gameplay relevance but is merely "frosting or eye-candy" to make the game "taste" better, it shouldn't be executed on the MMoG App server at all. **RIGHT?** Why should we add network lag and delay to sfx that do **NOT** impact other players?
- **Sound** — The Client-side plays all audio sound effects and/or music tracks. It is *preposterous* to think that the server would stream audio playback.
- **Input** — The Client-side collects a player's input, packages it, and then sends that information to the server in a negotiated

format. We'll study RPC or MOM **JSON declarative** formats in the upcoming Server and MMoG App chapters.

- *User Preferences* — Many games store user preferences on the local machine where the game runs. However, that also depends on the type of data. Obviously, a gamer's subscription account balance would be safely stored in the back-end business logic and storage. Safe data might be the gamer's native language, volume controls, and any keyboard adjustments.

- *Prediction* — The Client-side could predict what might happen to game objects in the short term while it awaits for the centralized server to synchronize and send "confirmations". I'll show you how this works later in this chapter using a client-side proxy server.

- *Interpolation* — As part of the Client-side prediction process, the Client can calculate where a game object needs to be, and where it thought it should be, and where the authoritative server confirms where it is, and shall go. Interpolation is important in "Real-time" games — when multiple players are simultaneously modifying the game state. Many MMoG tutorials don't tell you about "Separation of Concerns". The *"interpolation and extrapolation"* calculations are perfect candidates for a client-side proxy server.

Chapter 5 Exercise revisited: You'll recall that Colt McAnlis from Google Chrome Games (https://www.youtube.com/watch?v=Prkyd5n0P7k video 51:40; see 21:23 to 21:27) stated (quote), " . . . we're **going to ignore client-side prediction, is hands down, is the perceptive correct solution from all the game players.** If you're writing games, make sure you do this way."

The whole idea is amazing, that JavaScript can do all this locally. Then add onto this idea that JavaScript is based on a **single-threaded environment** that increases the "awesome factor". Web

Workers remove (partially) this single-threaded limitation as you've read in the previous MMoG Application Architecture chapter.

Testing Your Browser

As of 20190327, we know that over 95% of all browsers **already** support WebSockets **natively!** We should check if our browsers support WebSockets before we go any further writing our MMoG.

JS check for client-side WebSocket.

```
1     // Make sure the browser supports WebSocket
2     if (!window.WebSocket) {
3         displayMessage("Your browser does not support WebSockets");
4         return;
5     }
```

In your "Project Game Starter Kit", you downloaded earlier, search for the directory "WebSocket" and inside the "WebSocketTest.html" file and open it with your favorite browser. Click the link — "Run WebSocket" link. Testing completed. Did it work? Right? If not, then research https://canIuse.com at the bottom of the page are tabs leading to "Notes", "Known Issues", and current "Issues". You also might like to import their usage data and discover how much of the world already supports WebSockets **natively in browsers.** You also noticed that we didn't need a webserver to run this simple test; but, we will need a "full-stack" web server installed on our development workstation eventually.

NOTE: What you just did above is how your gamers will also enter your MMoG. **Study these files; it's just pure JavaScript** and **only your browser.** There's only the native WebSocket protocol; Socket.IO is **nowhere to be seen!** All the current MMoG tutorials spend half their time just getting Socket.IO up and running on your local workstation? **Why? Yeap,** we've already covered all those reasons in Part I, and now I'm demonstrating what I've claimed from those previous chapters.

Open the `WebSocketTest.html` and study what we just did. You may also test your active browser against either *my demo socket server* or against *websocket.org.* Review chapter 5 for other details:

Test sites:

https://mmog.pbmcube.net/index.php
https://websocket.org/demos.html
Client Interface:
http://www.abrandao.com/lab/websocket/client.html

WebSocket Protocol Handshake

To switch into an "upgraded WebSocket connection", the gamer's browser should send a ***"WebSocket handshake request",*** — which we did. The game testing servers will return a ***"WebSocket handshake response",*** — which it did; nothing new thus far . . . same old, same old that we studied in Parts I & II.

Deeper Dive: WebSocket API

Upgrade to WebSockets

The WebSocket API - Read more ...

Both server- and client-side WebSocket objects support the following API.

- ***on('open', function(event))*** fires when the socket connection is established. Event has no attributes. Ensure your data is sent only when a connection exists; we should wrap our `send()` method with an onopen event.
- ***on('message', function(event))*** fires when the socket receives a message. The "Event" has one attribute, data, which is either a String (for text frames) or a Buffer (for binary frames). The default data format is "blob" which is particularly useful when sending and receiving files.
- ***on('error', function(event))*** fires when there is a protocol error due to bad data sent by the other peer. This event is purely informational, you ***do not need*** to implement error recovery because WebSockets rides on top of TCP/IP. ***"So how do errors still creep in?"*** Superior question; the answer is found in *RFC 6455 Section 5.1 Overview* which you've already read (?) from the Networking Chapter exercises.
- ***on('close', function(event))*** fires when either the client or the server closes the connection conduit. This event has two

optional attributes — code and reason — that expose the status code and message sent by the peer that closed the connection. It also has three properties you can use for error handling and recovery: `wasClean`, `code`, and `error`.

- *send(message)* accepts either a String or a Buffer and sends a text or binary messages over the connection conduit to the other remote peer.
- *ping(message, function())* sends a "ping" frame with an optional message and fires the callback when a matching answer (aka "pong") is received. This is typically used to dynamically adjust the MMoG for network latency issues.
- *close(code, reason)* closes the connection conduit, sending the given status code and reason text, both of which are optional.
- *version* is a string containing the version of the WebSocket protocol the connection is using.
- *a protocol* is a string (which may be empty) identifying the sub-protocol the socket is using. We discuss various "sub-protocols" in the upcoming Server chapters.

The illustration above demonstrates the responsibilities of the client and the remote MMoG server on each end of the WebSocket communications conduit.

This line in our testing script
var ws = new WebSocket('ws://mmog.pbmcube.net:30113/', 'mmog');

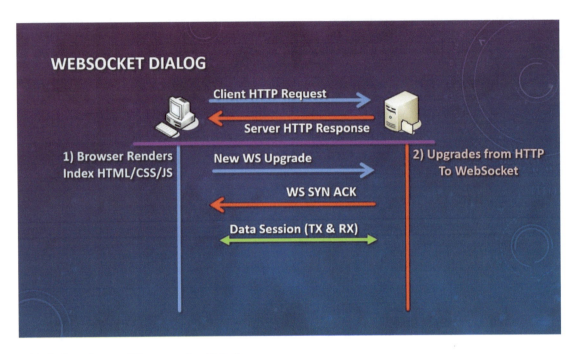

WebSockets Upgrade Dialog

Gamer's client requests above are similar to HTTP requests, each line ends with \r\n and there must be an extra blank line at the end. This is the standard format. The handshake resembles an HTTP request so that the game server can handle standard HTTP connections (port 80) as well as the new WebSocket connections across the same initial port 80 (or 443 for HTTPS). Once the new WebSocket request creates that connection, communications between the client and game server switches into a ***bidirectional binary protocol that does not conform*** to the former HTTP protocol. After a WebSocket connects, the gaming client and server can send WebSocket ***binary data or text frames*** in full-duplex mode — in either direction at the same time! This is a point-to-point connection as if the client and server were peers. The data is minimally framed (for us by the WebSocket Protocol) with just two bytes. (Review Chapter 3 Network Basics) There's no need to write code to package these frames as some tutorials lead us to believe. However, it is a "stream" of data; if your MMoG needs to understand discreet components, you might like to use a message format inside these WebSocket frames.

The WebSocket API allows for multiple types of data (`UTF8` text, `binary`, and `blob data`), and unlike the browser, these messages on the server are stored using different properties based upon those data types. In the case of text frames, each frame starts with a `0x00 byte`, ends with a `0xFF byte`, and contains `UTF-8` data in between. (Review Chapter 3 Network Basics page 62) This binary data stream is difficult for humans to read since it is a ***bidirectional binary protocol.*** WebSocket text frames use *a terminator,* while binary frames use a length prefix.

A typical Server's response header looks like this:

```
1    HTTP/1.1 101 Switching Protocols
2    Upgrade: websocket
3    Connection: Upgrade
4    Sec-WebSocket-Accept: cGxheWVyMzIxfGdhbWUxMjN8QUNL
5    Sec-WebSocket-Protocol: mmog, soap, wamp, sip, amqp, mqtt, xmpp
```

In addition to Upgrade headers, the client sends a `Sec-WebSocket-Key` header containing base64-encoded random bytes, and the server replies with a hash of the key in the `Sec-WebSocket-Accept` header. This is intended to prevent a caching proxy from re-sending any previous

WebSocket dialog, (see footnote 1) and ***does not provide any authentication, privacy, or integrity.*** The hashing function appends the fixed string `258EAFA5-E914-47DA-95CA-C5AB0DC85B11` (a GUID) to the value from `Sec-WebSocket-Key header` ***(which is not decoded from base64),*** applies the SHA-1 hashing function, and encodes the result using base64. (see footnote 2)

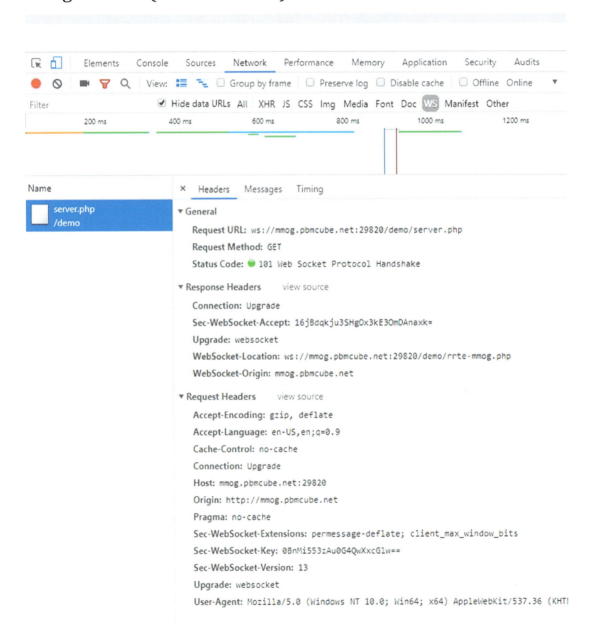

Observe WS Header Exchange in Developer Console

Launched the following

```
1       Request Headers . . .
2       GET ws://mmog.pbmcube.net:30113/demo/server.php HTTP/1.1
3       Host: mmog.pbmcube.net:30113
4       Connection: Upgrade
5       Upgrade: websocket
6       Origin: http://mmog.pbmcube.net
7       Sec-WebSocket-Version: 13
8       Sec-WebSocket-Key: zfG4XfYTSKp6NdIpCaYe+w==
9       Sec-WebSocket-Protocol: mmog, soap, wamp, sip, amqp, mqtt, xmpp
10      Sec-WebSocket-Extensions: permessage-deflate; client_max_window_bits
```

Exercise: WebSocket monitoring with *Wire-Shark in 3 min*

Observe these WebSocket frames with *Wire-shark.* (Refer to the Network Appendix on where to get **Wire-shark.**) Registered IANA Sec-WebSocket-Protocol is **referenced here.** The server can't send more than one `Sec-Websocket-Protocol` header. If the server doesn't want to use any sub-protocol, it shouldn't send any Sec-WebSocket-Protocol header. Sending a blank header is incorrect. The client may close the connection if it doesn't get the sub-protocol it wants.

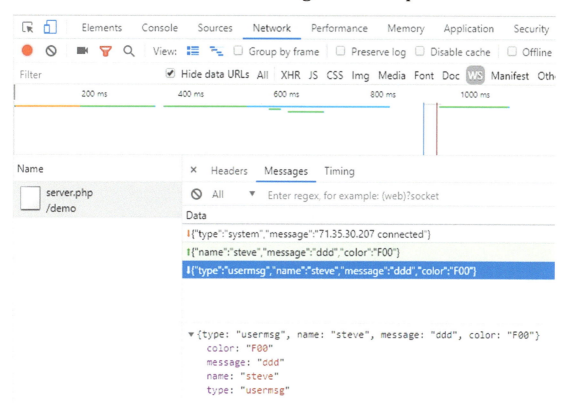

Observe WS Message Content Exchange in Developer Console

. . . and receives the following

```
1    Response Headers . . .
2    HTTP/1.1 101 Web Socket Protocol Handshake
3    Upgrade: websocket
4    Connection: Upgrade
5    WebSocket-Origin: mmog.pbmcube.net
6    WebSocket-Location: ws://mmog.pbmcube.net:30113/demo/rrte-mmog.php
7    Sec-WebSocket-Accept:EZtDpyc+cXnNbqdzXW1QCmdm//Y=
```

Exercise: Go back and re-do the browser test to either
mmog.pbmcube.net or websocket.org/demos.html. This time open your Develop
Console and observe your information headers and responses.
Exercise: Need help using the Developer Tools? With the Chrome
Dev Tools, you can now see the WebSocket traffic coming to and
going from your browser **without using tools like Wireshark.**
Review this article
https://developers.google.com/web/tools/chrome-devtools/

Note: Although the Web Sockets protocol is ready to support a
diverse set of clients beyond the gaming community, **it cannot
deliver raw binary data to JavaScript, because JavaScript does
not support a byte type.** Therefore, binary data is ignored if the
client is JavaScript — but raw binary data could be delivered to
other clients that support it; **the WebSocket protocol is platform-
independent.**

Sample Source Code: Client-side WebSocket

The client-side is easy; it's merely a JavaScript inside of an index
page. Once we know our MMoG App server is running — the remote
end of our WebSocket conduit — your gamers can connect to it
through your "Web Server" and "subscribe to gaming messages"
pushed from your MMoG App Server. The gamers will establish
WebSocket connections through a process known as "WebSocket
handshake". This "handshake" starts when the gamer visits a
"Game's index page" from the Web Server to enter a specific game. The
Web Server will then include an Upgrade header in this request that
tells the "MMoG App Server" a gamer wants to establish a

WebSocket connection. All of this was covered in Part I; this was simply a review.

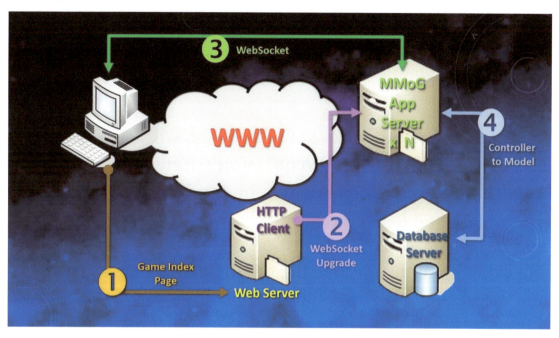

To Summarize into our 4-Step development process (Chapter 5)

1. ***Step #1:*** Inside the game's index page, create a JavaScript WebSocket object — it is the client-side conduit toward the MMoG server's URL.

2. ***Step #2:*** Generate code for the following events — ***"onopen"***, ***"onclose"***, and ***"onerror"*** as WebSocket event handlers. Construct the ***"onmessage"*** event handler (the client-side workhorse and potentially a proxy-server) to handle, deserialize, and read all incoming Game Turn Responses (GTR) coming from the MMoG App server.

3. ***Step #3:*** Sending Game Turn Orders (GTO) "messages" to the MMoG App server using the WebSocket send() method. This is the topic in later chapters and Part IV when we create Game Turn Orders and server's Game Turn Results.

4. ***Step #4:*** Closing the client-side WebSocket conduit connection to the MMoG App server using the WebSocket close() method and transition into a new game phase.

Using **HiveMQ,** you don't need a dedicated web-server in front of an MMoG App Server to forward the WebSocket connection. *Read more about HiveMQ ...*

WARNING: User agents must not convey any failure information to scripts in a way that would allow a script to distinguish the following situations:

- A server whose hostname could not be resolved.
- A server to which packets could not successfully be routed.
- A server that refused the connection on the specified port.
- A server that failed to correctly perform a TLS handshake (e.g., the server certificate can't be verified).
- A server that did not complete the opening handshake (e.g. because it was not a WebSocket server).
- A WebSocket server that sent a correct opening handshake, but that specified options that caused the client to drop the connection (e.g. the server specified a sub-protocol that the client did not offer).
- A WebSocket server that abruptly closed the connection after successfully completing the opening handshake.

In all of these cases, *the WebSocket connection close code* would be 1006, as required by the WebSocket Protocol specification. WSP

Allowing a script to distinguish these cases would allow a script to probe the user's local network in preparation for an attack. In particular, this means the `code 1015` is **not used** by the user agent (unless the server erroneously uses it in its close frame, of course).

Step #1: Game index page

Typical `index.html` with WebSocket

```
1    <!doctype html>
2    <html lang="en">
3    <head>
4      <meta charset="utf-8">
5      <link rel="dns-prefetch" href="http://mmog.pbmcube.net/">
```

```
 6        <title>WebSocket MMoG Client Example</title>
 7
 8        <!-- Typically Phaser Library is here with your gaming scripts -->
 9
10      </head>
11      <body>
12        <h1>MMoG Client-side via WebSockets</h1>
13        <p>Open the JavaScript console to see what's up!
14        Notice we're not using Node.js, Socket.IO; we're just
15        using your vanilla browser for now.</p>
16        <form>
17          <label for="message">Send a Game Turn</label>
18          <input id="message" name="message" type="text">
19          <button id="send" name="send">Submit</button>
20        </form>
21
22      <!-- The secret sauce is in this external file
23          or simply insert the script directly. -->
24        <script src="ws_client.js"></script>
25      </body>
26      </html>
```

This `index.html` file (above) is placed on the www server; it is sent to the gamer's browser. The client browser runs the JavaScript that will create the WebSocket conduit. This file is available in the "Project Game Starter Kit" at

- Download the *WebSockets.zip* **OR**
- Download the *MMoG server-side example*.

Step #2: Generate Event handlers

Let's turn our attention to that JavaScript just above the closing body tag. Initializing a WebSocket is just as simple as the following lines of JQuery code. Create an external file entitled `ws_client.js` or insert the following script directly into the `index.html` — search in your Bonus Content for the directory "/WebSockets/" and inside that for the `ws_client.js` *(click to review)* or *test online here:*

Testing a WebSocket script (ws_client.js)

```
1      (function () {
2          // --------------------------------
3          // You can check the number of bytes that have been
4          // queued but not yet transmitted to the server,
```

```
 5          // this is very useful if the client application transports
 6          // large amounts of data to the server.
 7          // --------------------------------
 8          var MAX_BUFFER = 8192;
 9
10          // --------------------------------
11          // Warning! NEVER USE WEBSOCKET 12345!
12          // port 12345 is a known virus;
13          // Read in Phaser Multi-Player Gaming Systems
14          // Chapter 6.2 WebSocket Protocol HandShake
15          // --------------------------------
16          // new WebSocket (url, optional sub-protocol)
17          var ws = new WebSocket('ws://localhost:12345', 'echo-protocol');
18
19          //============================
20          // Step 2: 4 WebSocket Protocol Msg
21          //============================
22          // WebSocket Events:
23          // you simply add callback functions to the WebSocket object
24          // or you can use the addEventListener() DOM method on your
25          // WebSocket objects. It's important to implement these events
26          //  before attempting to send any messages.
27          // --------------------------------
28          // Step #4: Close client-side conduit
29          // FIN finished and cleaning up connection.
30          ws.onclose = function (event) {
31              console.log('Connection closed.');
32          }
33
34          // Example of "close" addEventListner
35          // Set handler for when the socket connection is closed
36          // websocket.addEventListener("close", function() { ...}
37
38          // Oops! Discovered an error in the TCP/IP
39          //  overlooked RTT or RTO problems
40          // See RFC6455 Section 5.1 for more potential errors.
41          ws.onerror = function (event) {
42              console.log('An error occurred. Sorry for that.');
43          }
44          // --------------------------------
45
46          //Conversations/dialogs messages to and from
47          //  We'll cover this topic in later Chapters & Part IV.
48          // alternate method:
49          //      ws.onmessage = incomingMsg(event);
50          // Example of "message" addEventListner
51          // Set handler for when the socket receives a message
52          // websocket.addEventListener("message", function() { ...}
53          ws.onmessage = function (event) {
54              console.log('Response from server: ' + event.data);
```

```
55          }
56
57          ws.onopen = function (event) {
58              console.log('Connection opened.');
59              // let's try to send every second?
60              setInterval( function() {
61                  if (ws.bufferedAmount < MAX_BUFFER) {
62                      ws.send(checkTheStatusAndSendData());
63                  }
64              }, 1000);
65          }
66
67          // Add our customized handling
68          // The readyState attribute may have one of the four values:
69          // - CONNECTING (The connection is not yet fully open)
70          // - OPEN (The connection is open and ready to communicate)
71          // - CLOSING (The connection is in the process of closing)
72          // - CLOSED (the connection closed or couldn't be opened)
73          // Knowing the current state can be very useful in
74          // troubleshooting your application.
75          ws.sendMessage = function (message) {
76              if(ws.readyState === ws.OPEN){
77                  this.send(message);
78                  console.log('Message sent: ' + message);
79              } else {
80                  console.log('Connection failed.')
81              }
82          }
83
84          // Attach created game turn orders into a message frame
85          document.getElementById('send').addEventListener('click',
86          function (event) {
87              event.preventDefault();
88              var message = document.getElementById('message').value;
89              ws.sendMessage(message);
90          });
91
92      })();
```

Review the sample code above. It contains the WebSocket API in a few events — onclose, onerror, onmessage, and onopen. *That's it!* Sending messages to the server uses the method send() and disconnecting from the server uses the method close(). ***Why does everyone try to make this so difficult? AND! it's supported in 95% of all browsers NATIVELY!*** We managed to flip from an HTTP connection into a WebSocket connection using a simple upgrade command! Why was it so simple? Because both are "peer protocols" to each other riding above the TCP/IP transportation layer. Everything is explained in the *official W3C WebSocket API.* In Part I & II, we investigated that many other programming languages use this exact same WebSocket API specifications; without a doubt, WebSocket is *ubiquitous.*

In the code examples above, the `bufferedAmount` attribute is used to ensure that updates are sent at a rate of one update every 1000 ms (1 fps) if the network can handle that rate, or at whatever rate the network can handle, if that is too fast. The `bufferedAmount` attribute could saturate a network by sending data at a higher rate than the network can handle; this requires careful monitoring by using WebSocket "Pings" and "Pong" commands. We'll study and apply this information in upcoming server chapters.

Study `ws_client.js`*! There's no Socket.io, nor Node.js, nor Express.js!* We are using the internal native WebSocket protocol *already available inside our browsers. How easy was that? No extra code, no formatting the data stream, no encoding nor decoding, AND protocols are software language-agnostic!* Everything was already performed *for us by our browsers.* Furthermore, *Phaser — either version v2.x.x. or v3.16+ — had nothing to do with any of this;* the WebSocket conduit simply opened. Phaser is inside an HTML5 canvas tag (i.e., a Layer 7 application) — `Applications` receiving services from lower communication layers services (i.e., our WebSockets, and TCP/IP bindings), and let's keep it that way. This is the primary idea behind the concept of "Separation of Concerns" covered in both the *Phaser Game Design Workbook* and *Phaser Game Prototyping workbook, new 6th Edition*

WARNING: Do not use port 12345 as shown above; it appears as a Trojan Viruses: cron / crontab, Fat Bitch trojan, GabanBus, icmp_pipe.c, Mypic, NetBus, NetBus Toy, NetBus worm, Pie Bill Gates, Whack Job, X-bill. Click the link above to see all known port viruses. *Port 54321* in the example above is used by Back Orifice

2000 and School Bus viruses. **Research your port number selections wisely!**

If your ISP permits WebSockets or Node.js, they will assign you a software port number to use. *I'm fortunate to use an ISP* **that supports both Node.js and WebSockets.** Yes, Node.js can have a role in MMoG development if applied correctly as we learned in Part II. We covered all those "ins and outs" of Node.js and all the "whens and how-tos" previously.

Exercise: Research the other *WebSocket API attributes and commands* on Mozilla.

Exercise: Study *MDN: Writing WebSocket client applications* for more details.

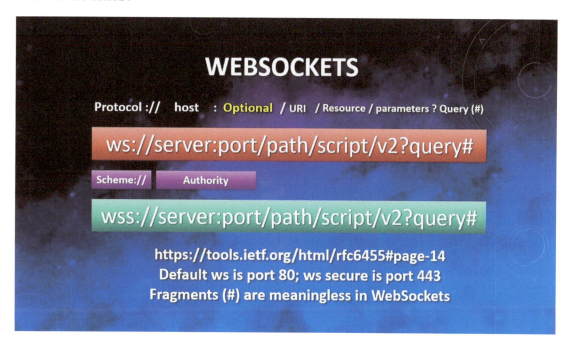

Server-side target

Exercise: Research the following and select, not less than 5 port nominations for your MMoG server. This will be useful if you are using Dockers, Kubernetes, or Cloud-based virtual environments.

- Trojan Port Table
- TCP & UDP ports for your online games

- Special Application Port List
- NMap Services
- Internet Storm Center
- Service Name and Transport Protocol Port Number Registry

Appendix: OLOO - Safe JavaScript

A Tutorial for Creating games in JavaScript using OLOO

An excerpt from *"JavaScript 'Objects Linking to Other Objects' (OLOO) in Game Development"* — a **FREE** online course for book patrons studying and contrasting *JS delegation vs OOP Inheritance.*

JS Objects: *"TL;DR"*

JavaScript has been plagued since the beginning with misunderstanding and awkwardness around its **"prototypal inheritance"** system, mostly because *"inheritance" isn't how JS works at all,* and trying to do that only leads to "gotchas" and "confusions" that we have to pave over with "user-land helper libraries". Instead, embracing that JS has "behavior delegation" — simple delegation links between objects — fits naturally with how JS syntax works, which creates more sensible code without the need for helpers. …

When you set aside distractions like *mixins*, *polymorphism,* composition, *classes,* constructors, and instances, **and only focus on** the objects that link to each other, you gain a powerful tool in behavior delegation that is easier to write, reason about, explain, and code-maintain. *Simpler is better.* JS is "objects-only" (OO). Leave the classes to those other languages! …

At this point of understanding, we should really ask ourselves: is the difficulty of *expressing classes and inheritance in pure JavaScript* a failure of the language (one which can *temporarily* be *solved* with *user libraries* and ultimately solved by *additions to the language* like `class { ...... }` syntax), as many game developers *feel,* or is it something deeper?

Is it indicative of a more fundamental disparity, that we're *trying to do something in JS* that it's *just not meant to do?*

JavaScript features stalled around 2007 to 2008; we've recently seen JavaScript language development making a fair amount of progress with promised releases every year (typically in June). In 2012, `Object.create` appeared in the standards. It allowed us to create objects with a selected prototype but didn't allow us to `get` nor `set` them. So, browsers implemented a non-standard `__proto__` accessor that permitted `getting` and `setting` a prototype at any time. Later in the year 2015, `Object.setPrototypeOf` and `Object.getPrototypeOf` were added to the standards. The `__proto__` was the "de-facto" — implemented everywhere — so, it made its way into the standard's Annex B — a description for optional non-browser environments.

The *ECMAScript 6-standard* is 4+ years old and *all major browsers currently support it (see this table).* The next *ECMA version* was ES6 (or ES2015, or "ESNext" (at that time), there are a lot of names for *JavaScript release versions*) that were only *partially supported by browsers back then.* However, since the ES5 specification is fully defined, software engineers wrote tools called *"transpilers"* — it takes ES6/7/8/9 formatted code and returns it into the standard ES5 code. You must be thinking, **"why would they do that?"** Because, it allows software engineers to use the newest released versions of the JavaScript specification and all the newest features; yet, still allows their code to be run in any browser. So, this is a perfect time to latch onto the new JS features and migrate to the modern style of game development using Phaser Gaming Frameworks v2.x.x and/or v3.x.x.

Before ECMAScript 6, there was a lot of confusion about how to use *Object Oriented Programming (OOP) in JavaScript;* the two methods used were either the *"factory pattern"* or the *"constructor function pattern".* ES6 added a new keyword to resolve this confusion and provide a single primary method to insert OOP into JS — the `class` keyword was introduced. Many believed, by adding this `class` keyword, it would solve many problems. In reality, it didn't! ***It simply poisoned the minds and added another layer of abstraction that misrepresented the JS prototype-based inheritance chain as masquerading as standard classic OOP inheritance.*** If you're using ES6 with classical Object-Oriented Programming, you will need a different structured approach known as ***Objects Linking to Other Objects (OLOO).*** Yes, there are many ways to style your JS source code. One prevalent way is to *shoehorn* JS into a ***Classical OOP format with inheritance;*** but, to do so is a misuse of the native objects and prototypical delegation found in the core of the JavaScript syntax. In fact, the *Gang of Four (GoF) states, "... favor object composition over class inheritance ...".* Read what Apple Game Develop says about *"Inheritance-Based Architecture Hinders Game Design Evolution"*

ES9 (June 2018) says this about OOP in JS, (quote pg 48), "... In a class-based object-oriented language, in general, 'state' is carried by instances, methods are carried by classes, and inheritance is only of structure and behavior. In ECMAScript, the state and methods are carried by objects, while structure, behavior, and state are all inherited. All objects that do not directly contain a particular property that their prototype contains share that property and its value."

Furthermore, "ES6 restricts what a `class` body content might contain." Quoted from Exploring ES6 by Dr. Axel Rauschmayer

15.2.2 Inside the body of a class definition

A class body can ***only contain methods, but not data properties.*** Prototypes having data properties is generally ***considered an anti-pattern,*** so this just enforces a best practice.

- ***3 Different Kinds of Prototypal Inheritance: ES6+ Edition*** by Eric Elliott.
- ***The Gang of Four is wrong and you don't understand delegation*** by Jim Gay.

The old way

Let's assume you're building a game studio/workshop and you need to create some release game products. In the old days (1997 to 2008) – **before ECMAScript 5 (ES5),** you would have written something like a function this way:

```
1    //"pseudo-constructor" JS Function; functions are "hoisted"
2    function game (name) {
3        this.name = name;
4    };
5
6    game.prototype.showName = function() {alert(this.name);};
7
8    ///////////////////////////////////////////////////
9    // OR when ES5 appeared, you may have shifted to an "object literal"
10   // "pseudo-constructor" JS object literal; object literals are
11   // NOT "hoisted".
12   ///////////////////////////////////////////////////
13    var game = functionName(name) {
14        this.name = name;
15   };
16
17   game.showName = function() {alert(this.name);};
18
19   //Phaser v2.x.x uses object literals with the "new" keyword.
20   var game = new Phaser.Game(640,450,Phaser.Auto,"gameDiv",boot);
21
22   document.addEventListerner('DOMContentLoaded',
23       function(){ window.game() );, false  });
```

This wasn't so bad. You have a function acting as a pseudo-*"constructor"* (an adopted terminology from OOP) to create your *game object singleton* and attach methods to the game's prototype. All individual games would have these methods. "Constructor functions" are technically just normal, old, regular functions — ***nothing more!*** For instance:

```
1    function User(name) {
2      this.name = name;
3      this.isAdmin = false;
4    }
5
6    let user = new User("Jack");
7
8    alert(user.name);        // Jack
9    alert(user.isAdmin);     // false
```

When *"new User(...)"* is called, it does several things:

- A new empty object was created.
- The *"this"* keyword was assigned to that newly created object. Additionally, the *"constructor"* property was changed to the parent function, and *"__proto__"* was set to that parent's *"constructor"* prototype. If no return value was set at the end of this function, then the function would return *"this"* — a reference to the object itself.
- The function body executes its statements and usually, it modifies this reference and adds other new properties into itself.
- The value of *"this"* was returned upon completion.

In other words, *"new User(...)"* really does something like this:

```
1    function User(name) {
2      // this = {};  (implicitly)
3
4      // add properties to this
5      this.name = name;
6      this.isAdmin = false;
7
8      // return this;  (implicitly)
9    }
10
11   //or something like this
12   var User = {
13       constructor:
14           this.name = name;
15           this.isAdmin = false;
16
17       //If we put methods here; every instance will use these
18       //   same methods.
19   }
```

However, there are several concepts to consider:

- There are **no private attributes** in the JavaScript language unless you choose to modify the `Object.defineProperty read-only` *into a `writable` flag to `false`.* **Be warned!** Once you change this, you **cannot** reverse your selection. The value inside a named variable can be changed at any time from outside its function; unless you set the property as "ready only".

- The **methods and properties are scattered**. Even if you put them all in one tight collection (aka a `class`), there is not a `single structure concept` to define your classic classful objects due to "hoisting" — just as you would do with classes in many other purely classical object-oriented languages. Objects use "values by reference".

- You might easily **forget to use the `new` keyword**. It doesn't throw an error and is perfectly acceptable in JS. It just leads to completely different behavior than you would expect and some nasty unintended bugs that become difficult to discover.

- **Classical OOP Inheritance** will provide further problems. There isn't an agreed-upon method in the JS-community about how to do this properly. In fact, in JS, *it is not inheritance at all (i.e., copying attributes and method into the `new` instance). Nothing in an object/function is "copied" in JavaScript.* When an object variable is copied — it's the reference (aka the memory address where the value lives) that is copied, *the object is not duplicated.*

If an internal property doesn't exist in an object, *JavaScript refers up the protocol chain to find it; it is "delegation".* John Dugan has an excellent illustration.

"Object-Oriented JavaScript Pattern Comparison"

"When your parents had you, you inherited their DNA — you *received a copy of it. When they broke their leg, yours did not break.* JavaScript is the opposite of this. In JavaScript, *when your*

parents break their leg, yours breaks too. A term better suited than prototypical inheritance to JavaScript is ***prototypical delegation.*** When a new object is created from another object in JavaScript, ***it links back to the parent object's prototype properties and methods as opposed to copying them."***

(Read more on this topic from, *"You don't know JS" Chapter 6*).

Here's a summary of the *Feature changes in ES6 here*)

A class with only a single instance with global access points.

```
1      // v2.x.x
2      var game = new Phaser.Game(480, 320, Phaser.AUTO, null, game.Boot);
3
4      // v3.x.x
5      var game = new Phaser.Game(config);   OR
6      var game = Object.assign({},Phaser.Game(config));   OR
7      var game.prototype = Object.create(Phaser.prototype);
```

When the new keyword is placed in front of any function call, four things happen:

1. A new object is created and assigned to the variable; new helps create an object from the parent function.
2. The new object gets linked to the parent object's prototype.
3. The new object gets associated with the keyword this within the constructor function call.
4. If the constructor function does not return a value, JavaScript ***implicitly inserts this context*** and returns it as a reference at the end of the constructor function's execution.

ECMA-262 7th Edition / June 2016

ECMAScript® 2016 Language Specification

(QUOTE) "A function object is an object that supports the [[Call]] internal methods. A constructor (also referred to as a constructor function) is a function object that supports the [[Construct]] internal method."

Refer to *Table 6*

... *A function object is not necessarily a constructor and such non-constructor function objects do not have a* `[[Construct]]` *internal method.*

Because of these points, many developers have created libraries, frameworks, and tools that provide all types of object creation and instantiation logic **to subjugate JS into the classical OOP comfort-zone.** Many of these "shackles", introduced by OOP classes (e.g. Prototype, ES6, TypeScript, LiveScript, or CoffeeScript), are nothing more than *"syntactic sugar" to fatten up* JS. I trust you haven't drunk this pre-sweetened "Kool-Aid"!? (oh! I offer my apology to those who've misunderstood my meaning).

You can skip down this yellow-brick road of classic OOP if you want, but I wouldn't recommend it because **your game will perform slower.** Test it for yourself; you'll see that *using OOP is 12% slower (click to see results) because of the hierarchy "tree walking".* It *may be hard to swallow (Kool-Aid reference above)*, yet prototypical delegation — Objects Linking to Other Objects (OLOO) — is much easier than classful-based OOP and provides additional further benefits. Just look at other prototypical languages such as *IO or Self.* These are an old pre-JavaScript syntax that made prototypes initially difficult to use.

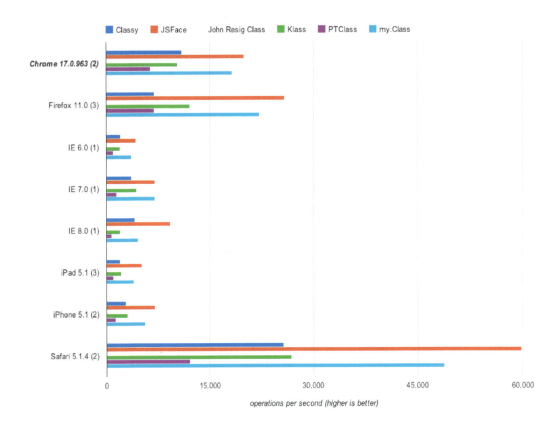

Comparison of JS OOP Class Systems

Douglas Crockford developed *this approach*. He wrote a short method — called `Object.create` — and it was adopted into the ES5 standards.

Objects Linking to Other Objects (OLOO)

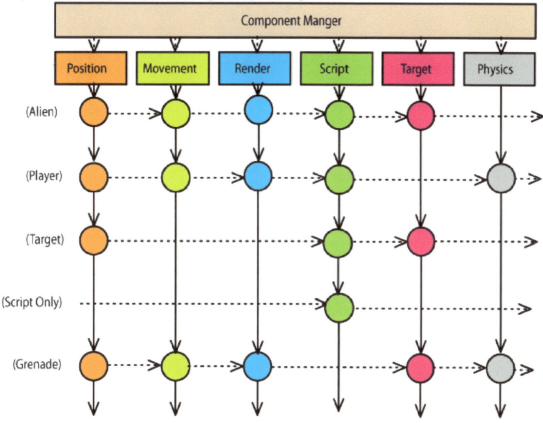

Figure 2   Object composition using components, viewed as a grid.

Entities and Component Game Design viewed as a cross-reference

In the OLOO style of creating objects, we strip away the "class" focus of objects typically seen in ES6 oriented programming and embrace the true nature of JavaScript's prototype features. In OLOO, objects delegate directly from other objects without needing to use a constructor as a middleman.

OLOO takes advantage of the Object.create method to take care of object creation and inheritance.

```
1    var myGame = {
2        init: function config(width, height) {
3            this.width = width;
4            this.height = height;
5        },
6
7        gameDim: function gameDim(config) {
```

```
 8              console.log('Dimensions: ' + this.width + 'x' + this.height);
 9          }
10      }
11
12      var gameCanvas = Object.create(myGame); //.init('800', '500');
13
14      //Debug Review
15      console.log("Game prototype (myGame): =======");
16      console.log("Match TYPE: "+myGame.isPrototypeOf(gameCanvas));
17      console.log("GET myGame: "+Object.getPrototypeOf(myGame));
18      console.log("myGame Properties: "+Object.values(myGame));
19      console.log("End of (myGame): =======");
```

Read more on other Object properties here.

Compare your code

You can check the finished code for this lesson in the live demo below, and run it to understand how it works:

https://makingbrowsergames.com/jsoloo/index-OLOO.pdf

Object.create

But what does Object.create do exactly? How is it different from OOP constructors?

Object.create is like an OOP constructor in that it creates a new object from the referenced object passed into it and builds a chain (aka inherits). In other words, it changes the value of __proto__ on the newly created object pointing to the object referenced. However, the true advantage of Object.create is its emphasis on prototype chains and delegation. To get a better idea of what Object.create does, you can rewrite it as a new function:

```
1      function createObject(obj) {
2          var newObj = {};            //new object created
3          newObj.__proto__ = obj;   //chain to properties of referenced obj
4          return newObj;                      //return "THIS" newObj reference
5      }
```

As you can see (in the code above), the new object (newObj) created doesn't have properties nor method behaviors. It inherits all of those from the referenced object handed in as an argument. If we should call any method on this new bare object, our program would find that method following the __proto__ property (instead of inside the object itself).

However, if you plan to create unique properties for this object, you need to create an `initialize` method as in the former example using `config`.

There is a drawback for `Object.create`. It doesn't allow you to use `instanceof` for quick "inheritance" checks **because it doesn't touch the constructor property.** Instead, to check for an inheritance, you use the `.isPrototypeOf` method on the originally referenced object.

The good news is that you don't need a modern browser with any ES5 implementation. Mozilla Developer Network provides a polyfill. It allows you to use this way of creating objects **since 2011, even inside older browsers.** But before you get all happy with this free gift, refer to https://caniuse.com/#search=ES5 and update your information — today this is not an issue anymore. This is important, considering the adoption trends of browsers. It is not an issue if you only target Firefox, Chrome, Safari, or Opera users. If you have doubts, research this compatibility chart or go to http://canIuse.com.

```
1    //Mozilla Polyfill:
2    if (! Object.create) {
3        Object.create = function (o) {
4            if (arguments.length &gt; 1) {
5                throw new Error('Object.create implementation
6                only accepts the first parameter.');
7            }
8        }
9    }
10
11   function F() {
12       F.prototype = o;
13       return new F();
14   };
```

You will have a function for the Object.create by just including the above source code. The first line checks whether `Object.create` exists already. ***This ensures that it won't override any native implementation should the browser produce one.***

Basic Syntax:

Object.create(prototype_object, propertiesObject)

Exercise Lesson 9:

1. The issues derive from writing source code in ES6 and using transpilers; don't believe me?? Research and record information from here

   ### ***Instructions:***
   - Click on the "6" or "2016+" tab at the top of the page.
   - Find the "Syntax" in the Feature Name column and then drop-down "default function parameters" Slide down the new list that appears and find "**new** Function() support"

   Record which compilers/polyfills support the "new Function()" feature.

2. Record which compilers/polyfills support the "new.target" feature.

3. Record which compilers/polyfills support the Functions "class" feature.

4. Record which compilers/polyfills support the Functions "super" feature.

5. Do any compilers/polyfills support Annex b.

   How many total features are supported by:

   a. TypeScript + core.js;
   b. Babel 6 or 7 + core.js

Game Singletons

"Let's take another look at our Phaser game project. If you would like to create only one game, there is no need for Object.create. Just create the object directly. ***All JS objects are "singletons".*** A Singleton is a class with only a single instance with global access points. In my example below, you don't need (and cannot) create an instance of the game object (mistaken for a class), it already exists. "... So, you simply start using the instance. In "classical" languages such as Java, singleton means that you can have only one single instance of this class at any time, you cannot create more objects of the same class. However, in JavaScript (no classes, remember?) this concept makes no sense anymore since all objects are singletons to begin with." quoted from Stoyan Stefanov — a Facebook engineer and O'Reilly author

```
1      // creates our game name-space
2      var game = {} || game;
3
4      /**
5      ////////////////////////////////////////////
6      // PHASER v2.x.x
7      ////////////////////////////////////////////
8      // using traditional new keyword found in all Phaser Tutorials
9
10     game = new Phaser.Game(
11         this.viewportWidth,
12         this.viewportHeight,
13         Phaser.AUTO,
14         document.body,
15         window.GAMEAPP.state.boot);
16
17     */
18
19     // main function - using Object.create
20     main: function(){
21         //game IS Phaser!!
22         game = Object.create(Phaser);
23     },
24
25     ////////////////////////////////////////////
26     // NEW Phaser v3.x.x method
27     ////////////////////////////////////////////
28     //     passing via Object.create
```

```
29      //    config submitted as an external object
30      main: function(){
31          this.game = Object.create(Phaser);
32      },
33
34
35      /**
36      // config object embedded into Phaser v3 instantiation
37      this.game = new Phaser.Game(
38          //configuration object submitted to Phaser v3
39          {
40              type: Phaser.AUTO,
41              parent: document.body,
42              scene: [],
43              width: window.Game.viewportWidth,
44              height: window.Game.viewportHeight
45          }
46      );
47      */
```

Download the *main.js* example file.

However, this isn't our best solution. You might manipulate those properties inside the object easily from the outside and there are no precautions for the assigned values. Take into consideration an assignment like a game.price = -20. A mistake like this would ensure the sale of your game products quickly with really happy customers — customers who receive $20 bucks from you with every game purchased. Your studio wouldn't be able to do that for very long!

Years of experience in object-oriented programming and design tells us to separate the **inner states** of an object from its **outer interfaces**. You usually want to make your game attributes private and provide some protection methods.

Deeper Dive: Object Manipulation objects in ES5/6

Objects get a major overhaul in ES6. Things like object destructuring and rest/spread operators made working with objects very easy. Let's jump to the code and try to merge two objects in ES5.

```
1      var obj1 = { a: 1, b: 2 }
2      var obj2 = { a: 2, c: 3, d: 4}
3      var obj3 = Object.assign(obj1, obj2)
```

We have to merge the object using Object.assign() which takes both objects as input and outputs the merged object. Let's take a look at how we can tackle this problem in ES6.

```
1    const obj1 = { a: 1, b: 2 }
2    const obj2 = { a: 2, c: 3, d: 4}
3    const obj3 = {...obj1, ...obj2}
```

Simple isn't it? The spread operator makes merging objects a breeze for the developer. But how does that apply to Phaser v2.x.x or III? Well, you've noticed by now that there are segregated `preload`, `config`, `create`, and `updates` function along with the global window. why not simply write them once and **"Merge"** them like this.

```
1    var preload = { loads all game assets };
2    var create = { assigns cached assets to scene }
3
4    var GameMechanics = Object.assign(preload, create);
5    var scene1 = Object.assign(GameMechanics,Phaser.Scene);
```

Lesson Summary

As of 20180720, "328 out of 330 liked/approved" this answer provided on *Understanding the difference between Object.create() and new SomeFunction()*

> (Quote) "Very simply said, `new X` is `Object.create(X.prototype)` with additionally running the constructor function. (And giving the constructor the chance to return the actual object that should be the result of the expression instead of this.)
>
> That's it. :)
>
> The rest of the answers are just confusing **because apparently nobody else reads the definition of** `new` **either. ;)"**

Resource References:
- *Not Awesome ES6 Classes*
- *How to fix the ES6 class keyword*
- *ECMA-262 7.0*

- http://www.crockford.com/javascript/inheritance.html
- http://crockford.com/javascript/

Notes

Making HTML5 Games

Introduction to Game Design

1Gose, S. (2016, November 8). Phaser Game Design Workbook. (6th Edition) Retrieved from https://leanpub.com/phaserjsgamedesignworkbook. ↵

2Gose, S. (2016, August 5). Phaser Game Prototyping Workbook. (6th Edition) Retrieved September 04, 2017, from https://makingbrowsergames.com/book/. ↵

3Gose, S. (2013, December 18). Phaser Making Massive Multi-Player Online Games (MMoG). (5th Edition) Retrieved September 04, 2017, from https://makingbrowsergames.com/mmog/. ↵

Standard Project Setup

1Now might be a good time to review what the *US Copyrights & Patent Office* **says about game ideas.** ↵

Starting a Game Project

1No, it **does NOT have to be written** in JavaScript. We could deliver these game phases as separate web pages generated from our back-end software (i.e., Python, PHP, Node.js, .NET, etc)↵

Part II: Making *"Collapsing Blocks"* Browser Games

Collapsing Blocks — Core Game Construction

1Cocoon was a powerful tool when combined with GUI-editors and *Cocoon Mobile Development*. (See *Migration guide* from Cocoon.js to Cordova/PhoneGap).↩

2Refer to https://en.wikipedia.org/wiki/Flood_fill for 5 pseudo code variations. ↩

3Juul, Jesper. "Swap Adjacent Gems to Make Sets of Three: A History of Matching Tile Games". Artifact journal. Volume 2, 2007. London: Routledge. http://www.jesperjuul.net/text/swapadjacent ↩

4You'll find that for the past decade game developers are using "Entities and Components" in game design. Read what Apple Game Development says about OOP in their section guides: 1) **"Inheritance-Based Architecture Hinders Game Design Evolution"** and; 2) **"Composition-Based Architecture Makes Evolving Game Design Easy".** ↩

Conclusion

1JavaScript Modules Part 2: Module Bundling – freeCodeCamp (2016, February 05). Retrieved September 04, 2017, from https://medium.freecodecamp.org/javascript-modules-part-2-module-bundling-5020383cf306 ↩

Answers to Exercises

Appendix

Appendix: OLOO - Safe JavaScript